D0207609

BANKING ACROSS
STATE LINES

BANKING ACROSS STATE LINES

Public and Private Consequences

Peter S. Rose

QUORUM BOOKS
Westport, Connecticut • London

Library of Congress Cataloging-in-Publication Data

Rose, Peter S.
   Banking across state lines : public and private consequences /
Peter S. Rose.
      p.   cm.
   Includes bibliographical references and index.
   ISBN 1–56720–007–9 (alk. paper)
   1. Interstate banking—United States—State supervision.
   2. Interstate banking—Law and legislation—United States.
   I. Title.
   HG2491.R648   1997
   332.1′6—dc20   96–46085

British Library Cataloguing in Publication Data is available.

Library of Congress Catalog Card Number: 96–46085
ISBN: 1–56720–007–9

First published in 1997

Quorum Books, 88 Post Road West, Westport, CT 06881
An imprint of Greenwood Publishing Group, Inc.

Printed in the United States of America

The paper used in this book complies with the
Permanent Paper Standard issued by the National
Information Standards Organization (Z39.48–1984).

10 9 8 7 6 5 4 3 2 1

To My Family

Contents

Tables

Preface

Federal Reserve Board Chairman Alan Greenspan in a speech to the Conference of State Bank Supervisors in April 1994 observed: "I am often bemused when both foreign and American observers compare the U.S. and foreign banking structures, note the uniqueness of the American System and conclude that since the American banking system is so different it should be changed. . . . Our banking system is, in fact, the envy of the world, in part because of its ability to rebound from crises that may well have devastated more rigid banking systems."

Dr. Greenspan's statement is still true as far as it goes, but what he (probably unintentionally) left out of the story is that American banking is being inexorably pushed by economic forces and government regulations towards a system that looks increasingly like the British and the Canadians and most other banking systems around the world—a handful of dominating banks operating hundreds, if not thousands, of branch offices and affiliated businesses worldwide. Industry statistics tell the story: (1) the total number of U.S. banks has fallen in less than ten years from more than fourteen thousand to less than ten thousand; (2) the number of independently owned banks has fallen by more than 20 percent over the same period; (3) branch offices of existing banks have soared to more than sixty-five thousand and automated teller machines (ATMs) in stores and shopping centers now exceed one hundred thousand; (4) in only fifteen years, from 1980 to 1995, forty-nine states passed legislation allowing banking firms from other states to enter their territory; (5) more than three hundred interstate companies now control over a quarter of U.S. domestic deposits, a percentage that has tripled in less than a decade; (6) the one hundred largest U.S. banks now account for more than 70 percent of the public's deposits compared to less than 50 percent in 1980; and finally (7) in more than a dozen states interstate banking firms now control half or more of the public's deposits.

In brief, American banking has entered an era of *accelerating consolidation of the banking businesses*—a trend toward many fewer but much more dominating banking firms. With the passage of sweeping federal legislation in 1994, the process of crossing state lines with full-service branches can begin legally in 1997—something that federal law and the laws of most states have expressly forbidden for half a century or more. The key issue for the public and for bankers themselves is: *What does this mean for customers and for the banks they patronize?* Do the claims of interstate banking's proponents— greater customer convenience through easier access to financial services (especially for the roughly sixty million people who live in one state and commute to work in another), more and improved financial services, greater bank safety and stability, and more efficient regulation and control—have any evidence to support them?

And what of the potential costs and disadvantages? Without argument, the public's deposits are being concentrated in fewer banks at both national and state levels and the service fees reported in recent national surveys of the industry are rising. What happens to bank stockholders and employees when these takeovers occur? Will the outcome be like the huge Bank-America-Security Pacific merger that resulted in about three thousand fewer employees and close to five hundred fewer full-service offices to serve the public? What about the states who could lose millions of dollars in tax revenues as local banking firms are consolidated into interstate companies headquartered in only a handful of states (including California, New York, North Carolina, Florida, Massachusetts, Minnesota, Ohio, Illinois, and Wisconsin)? And what about small banks, who will be almost certainly under greater and greater pressure to survive? What are their chances for success in the future?

This book examines these and other issues in seven chapters. The initial chapter examines the global uniqueness of the current U.S. banking industry and how the American banking structure has changed since 1980. The forces behind these changes—bank failures, poorly designed and implemented regulations, shifting population, intense financial-services competition, and financial pressures inside banks themselves—are discussed here. The chapter assesses where the U.S. banking structure seems to be going and whether, as some believe, traditional banks are slowly dying, beaten down by competition for customers by mutual funds, insurance companies, pension funds, and other aggressive financial-service providers.

Chapter 2 provides some essential background to the newest industry changes by looking at the history of American banking legislation, most notably the story behind the passage of the historic McFadden-Pepper, Glass-Steagall, and Bank Holding Company Acts at the federal level. It also examines the interstate banking laws of each of the fifty states and what factors motivated their passage. Competition between the states and real economic distress have played major roles in the interstate movement.

Chapter 3 explores the terms of the sweeping interstate banking law passed by the U.S. Congress in August of 1994 and in the same year signed into law by President Clinton in September. The chapter reviews the support and the opposition for this law and what changes it may bring to individual states. The 1994 banking legislation also offered the first regulatory relief to the industry after more than a decade of stronger government control over bank operations, service options, and capital. The probable impact of these newer and more liberal regulatory rules is assessed.

Chapter 4 addresses the alleged benefits and costs of interstate banking and evaluates these projected advantages and disadvantages in the light of existing evidence. Among the key issues here are claims of greater service convenience, broader service menus, greater service innovation, improved bank safety, and greater regulatory efficiency. The countervailing costs may include greater concentration of the public's deposits and industry resources, higher service fees, abnormal returns flowing to the stockholders of acquired banking firms but not necessarily to acquiring firm shareholders, loss of state tax revenues, loss of industry jobs, branch closings, failures among predominantly small local banks, and loss of local control over loan decisions.

Chapter 5 is particularly important to the book because it examines the research evidence bearing on the claims of both opponents and proponents of interstate banking. Separate sections of the chapter will explore the consequences of interstate banking for bank shareholder returns, bank risk exposure, and operating efficiency; for competition among financial-service providers; for customer convenience; and for the important issue of bank safety and soundness. A key question here is whether bank geographic diversification across state lines can reduce the risks carried by individual banking firms.

Chapter 6 looks at how bankers choose their target market areas and target banking firms to acquire across state lines. It assesses the quality of the factors bankers examine when selecting cities and towns to enter and examines the characteristics of banks targeted for acquisition by interstate banking companies.

The book concludes with Chapter 7, which explores how the U.S. banking structure is likely to change with the spread of interstate banking and what consequences the interstate movement would seem to have for the public, bank regulators, and the bankers themselves. Special attention is focused on the probable consequences of the interstate movement for service availability, service pricing, the safety and stability of American banks, and for the competitiveness of American banks abroad.

CHAPTER 1

The Old and the New: American Banking in Consolidation

THE GLOBAL UNIQUENESS OF THE AMERICAN BANKING INDUSTRY

The American banking industry is one of the most diverse banking systems in the world. It is, on the one hand, dominated numbers-wise by thousands of small, locally owned institutions but, on the other hand, dominated resource-wise by a handful of banks whose names are known and respected all over the globe. In America, as in no other place on the planet, banking is open both to the smallest and largest financial-service companies despite the impression people may sometimes receive from the industry's leaders and their almost daily announcements of mergers. In fact, many of the smallest American banks outperform the biggest in the industry in earnings, stability of return, portfolio quality, and operating efficiency. Nearly everywhere else on the planet, banks are large and dominating corporations, owning as well as lending to other corporate giants, and many are government owned or government controlled (such as France's Banque National de Paris and Credit Lyonnais).

This uniqueness in the structure of one of the most vital of all American industries reflects, in part, the unique origins of the United States itself. Founded as a nation of farmers, ranchers, and owners of small, family-owned businesses, public fear of concentrated banking power led to a welter of state laws and regulations, later joined by even more stringent federal rules, which limited both bank size and territorial aggressiveness. The basic idea behind these dual federal and state rules is painfully transparent: Keep American banks relatively small and principally dependent upon the goodwill and financial support of their local customers. Such a regulatory regime should insure that the *local* consumer of banking services will remain in charge. Moreover, few banks will be able to grow large enough to dominate and eliminate their competitors. Most American banking firms will be forced to listen to the financial-service demands of their local customers—predominantly households and small businesses—who will be assured of an adequate and reliable supply of credit and financial expertise.

THE U.S. BANKING STRUCTURE BETWEEN 1980 AND NOW

Despite the widespread public perception of American banking as a home-grown, predominantly small unit industry, however, the fundamental character of the United States' banks is changing rapidly and profoundly today. In no period of banking's history has this been more evident than in the years since 1980, when a strong *consolidation* trend began to reshape American banking into something quite new.

One of the most dramatic changes is an accelerating decline in the number of separately incorporated banks. As table 1.1 shows, the number of operating banks in the United States has fallen more than 30 percent since 1980 and by nearly one-fifth between 1990 and 1995 alone. There are now fewer independent U.S. banking firms (not affiliated through common ownership ties with other banking firms) than at any other time in the twentieth century. In fact, the number of independent American banking firms fell by nearly 40 percent between 1980 and 1995 and by more than 16 percent just since 1990. The number of full-service banking offices rose rapidly until the 1990s but then began to level out in the 1990s under the combined onslaught of cost-cutting measures and the substitution of automation—computer and telephone banking services—for live bank personnel. Still, Americans appear to be about as conveniently served as they were a decade ago with only about four thousand people per banking office—about the same ratio as in Western Europe.

One of the driving forces behind these remarkable changes is a merger and acquisitions wave of unprecedented proportions, resulting in more than sixty-three hundred banks being acquired or merged since 1980—an average of over four hundred per year—and giving rise to new industry leaders to stand beside and, in some cases, eclipse the traditional trendsetters. As table 1.2 relates, well over a trillion dollars in banking industry assets have been merged or acquired since 1980, representing almost 80 percent of the industry's total assets in current dollars. The banks most involved in these well-publicized recent merger and acquisition combinations include such

Table 1.1

Number of U.S. Commercial Banks, Banking Organizations, and Offices, 1980–95[1]

Year	Banks[2]	Banking Organizations[2]	Number of Banking Offices[3]	Population Per Banking Office[4]
1980	14,407	12,335	52,710	4,307
1981	14,389	12,177	54,734	4,184
1982	14,406	11,924	53,826	4,310
1983	14,405	11,669	55,109	4,246
1984	14,381	11,353	56,051	4,211
1985	14,268	11,019	57,417	4,145
1986	14,052	10,510	58,182	4,125
1987	13,542	10,099	58,521	4,114
1988	12,967	9,719	59,569	4,113
1989	12,556	9,457	61,219	4,035
1990	12,195	9,224	63,393	3,928
1991	11,791	9,010	64,681	3,896
1992	11,350	8,734	65,122	3,916
1993	10,869	8,324	63,658	4,053
1994	10,362	7,901	65,100	3,994
1995	10,083	7,715	n.a.	n.a.

Notes:

[1] Banks are defined as insured commercial banks; banking organizations are defined as bank holding companies and independent commercial banks; and banking offices are defined as insured U.S. commercial banks plus branch offices owned by insured U.S. commercial banks.

[2] Based upon Reports of Condition and Income, filed by U.S. banks with their principal federal supervisory agency.

[3] Number of banking offices = number of insured U.S. commercial banks + number of branches owned by insured U.S. commercial banks. The source of the branch figures is the *Annual Statistical Digest* published by the Board of Governors of the Federal Reserve System, with preliminary data for 1994.

[4] Population data for 1980–93 are from the U.S. Department of Commerce (Bureau of Economic Analysis). The 1994 data are estimated.

Source: Reported in Janet L. Yellen, Testimony before the Subcommittee on Financial Institutions and Consumer Credit, U.S. House of Representatives, October 17, 1995.

leading companies as Chemical Banking Corp. of New York, Chase Manhattan Corporation, BancOne Corp., Bank of America, First Union and First Fidelity Corporation, Fleet Financial Group, First Interstate Bancorp, Nations Bank, Norwest Corporation, Key Corp, First Chicago Corp, NBD Bancorp, Inc., Barnett Banks, Inc., Comerica Inc., and Wells Fargo, to name just a few. Indeed, this latest merger trend is marked by record numbers of very large merger transactions, well beyond the size of any previous megamergers in the nation's history.

A significant portion of the consolidation trend in American banking might not have taken place had it not been for the industry's serious loan quality and earnings problems of the 1980s and early 1990s. The rate of

Table 1.2
U.S. Commercial Bank Mergers and Holding Company Acquisitions,
1980–94

Year	Number of Bank Mergers	Bank Assets Acquired ($ Billions)
1980	190	$ 10.18
1981	359	34.07
1982	420	40.87
1983	428	50.05
1984	441	69.82
1985	475	67.12
1986	573	94.41
1987	649	123.29
1988	468	87.71
1989	350	43.39
1990	366	43.74
1991	345	150.29
1992	401	165.42
1993	436	103.05
1994	446	111.76
Total	6,347	1,195.17

Sources: Stephen A. Rhoades, "Mergers and Acquisitions by Commercial Banks, 1980–1994,"
Staff Study, Federal Reserve Board, 4th quarter 1995; and Janet L. Yellen, Testimony
before the Subcommittee on Financial Institutions and Consumer Credit, U.S. House of
Representatives, October 17, 1995.

bank failures during the 1980s represented the greatest number of bank
closings, on a year-by-year basis, since the Federal Deposit Insurance Corporation was founded in 1934. As table 1.3 relates, just over fifteen hundred
U.S.-insured banks failed between 1980 and 1995. While *new* bank formations more than made up for those failing and leaving the industry, the
industry's potent merger and acquisitions trend overwhelmed the numbers
of new bank charters, sharply driving down the industry's population of
functioning firms.

Moreover, as the 1990s loomed on the horizon, bank branch office closings began to approach new branch office openings, in part because advancing technology has reduced the need for so much physical proximity to
the customer and because recent mergers have brought together many banks
with overlapping and duplicate facilities. Indeed, the merger wave that has
swept through U.S. banking since 1980 may be viewed as a response to
"excess capacity" in an industry whose basic services have recently been
copied by hundreds of nonbank and foreign competitors. As Federal Reserve
Board economist Stephen A. Rhoades (1996) has recently noted, mergers

Table 1.3
Entry and Exit in U.S. Commercial Banking, 1980–95

| Year | New Banks | Number | | | |
		Failure of FDIC-Insured Banks	Mergers and Acquisitions	Bank Branches Openings	Closings
1980	206	10	190	2,397	287
1981	199	10	359	2,326	364
1982	316	42	420	1,666	443
1983	366	48	428	1,320	567
1984	400	79	441	1,405	889
1985	318	120	475	1,480	617
1986	248	138	573	1,387	763
1987	212	184	649	1,117	960
1988	234	200	468	1,676	1,082
1989	204	206	350	1,825	758
1990	165	168	366	1,987	926
1991	106	124	345	2,788	1,456
1992	96	120	401	1,755	1,435
1993	76	42	436	1,909	1,493
1994	66	13	446	2,461	1,146
1995	125	—	—	2,367	1,319
Total	3,337	1,504	6,347	30,866	14,505

Sources: Failure data are from *Annual Report* of the Federal Deposit Insurance Corporation and statistical releases. Mergers and acquisitions data are from Stephen A. Rhoades, "Mergers and Acquisitions by Commercial Banks, 1980–94," *Staff Study,* Federal Reserve Board, 4th quarter 1995. New bank and branch openings and closings are from the Federal Reserve Board, *Annual Statistical Digest,* relevant years; and Janet L. Yellen, Testimony before the Subcommittee on Financial Institutions and Consumer Credit, U.S. House of Representatives, October 17, 1995.

are one way for any industry to rid itself of overbuilding in service facilities and producing units.

INTERSTATE BANKING'S ROLE IN THE CONSOLIDATION AND CONCENTRATION OF AMERICAN BANKING

What role has interstate banking played in this sea of change sweeping through America's banking industry? Without question the spread of *interstate* banking has been a big part of the ongoing consolidation trend in American banking. As recently as 1987 there were only fifty-one bank holding companies controlling one or more banks across state lines, and these firms represented just 6 percent of all domestic commercial bank assets. By June 30, 1993 (as calculated by Savage [1993]), however, the number of interstate banking firms had more than tripled, rising to 178 companies,

Table 1.4
Shares of Domestic Commercial Banking Assets Held by the Largest Banking
Organizations Operating in the United States, 1980–95

Year	Top 5	Top 10	Top 25	Top 50	Top 100
1980	13.5	21.6	33.1	41.6	51.4
1981	13.2	21.1	33.2	41.6	51.6
1982	13.7	21.8	34.2	43.0	53.6
1983	13.2	21.0	34.0	43.3	54.3
1984	13.0	20.4	33.3	43.7	55.4
1985	12.8	20.4	33.2	45.8	57.9
1986	12.7	20.2	34.1	47.3	60.4
1987	12.6	19.9	34.8	48.5	61.9
1988	12.8	20.4	35.7	51.1	64.0
1989	13.3	21.7	36.9	51.8	64.7
1990	13.1	21.8	37.8	52.7	65.4
1992	16.0	24.4	40.3	53.4	65.5
1992	17.3	25.6	41.8	55.6	67.1
1993	17.6	26.9	43.8	58.0	69.2
1994	18.2	27.9	45.7	59.9	71.3
June 1995	17.6	27.1	45.3	60.0	71.5

Sources: NIC Database, Reports of Condition and Income; and Janet L. Yellen, Testimony
before the Subcommittee on Financial Institutions and Consumer Credit, U.S. House of
Representatives, October 17, 1995.

holding just over 21 percent of all domestic banking assets, and claiming close
to 23 percent of all domestic U.S. deposits. In thirteen states, interstate banking firms accounted for half or more of all deposits in those states by the mid-
1990s. More recently, Federal Reserve Board member Janet Yellen (1995)
finds that, as of June 1995, out-of-state banking organizations had risen to
control an average of 27 percent of all domestic bank deposits per state.

Clearly, while still in the minority, the share of industry resources controlled by interstate banking companies is advancing rapidly. Moreover, due
to recent changes in federal and state laws, the vast majority of domestic
banks now are open to acquisition by out-of-state banking companies. After
September 19, 1995, well-capitalized and well-managed bank holding companies could acquire banks in any state in the nation under the terms of the
1994 Riegle-Neal Interstate Banking and Branching Efficiency Act (to be
discussed later).

Not surprisingly, with the recent waves of acquisitions and failures, the
nationwide concentration of U.S. banking resources has been deepening at
a record pace. As table 1.4 shows, by mid-1995 the one hundred largest
U.S. banking organizations accounted for almost 72 percent of all domestic
bank assets, compared to little more than 50 percent in 1980. The top fifty
banks have jumped from holding about 40 percent of industry assets to
commanding close to 60 percent of the industry's resources. Instead of tra-

Table 1.5
The Largest Interstate Banking Organizations in the United States, 1993

Interstate Banking Organization	Home State	Number of Different States in Which Interstate Organization Controls Insured Commercial Banks	Proportion of Each Bank Holding Company's Domestic Deposits Coming From Outside Its Home State (percent)	Total Domestic Deposits (in billions of dollars)
BankAmerica Corp.	California	9	26.2%	$123.7
Nations Bank Corp.	North Carolina	11	90.4	82.6
Chemical Banking Corp.	New York	4	27.9	74.1
BancOne Corp.	Ohio	8	48.1	69.4
Citicorp	New York	9	27.0	48.7
First Interstate Corp.	California	13	61.3	43.5
Chase Manhattan Corp.	New York	7	27.1	40.0
First Union Corp.	North Carolina	6	71.0	38.2
Barnett Banks	Florida	2	3.4	34.6
Fleet Financial Group, Inc.	Rhode Island	6	83.6	32.3
PNC Financial Corp.	Pennsylvania	6	29.3	29.4
NBD Bancorp	Michigan	5	48.0	29.3
Sun Trust Banks, Inc.	Georgia	3	72.7	29.0
Norwest Corp.	Minnesota	11	60.9	27.0
Mellon Bank Corp.	Pennsylvania	3	3.5	24.1
Wachovia Corp.	North Carolina	4	50.7	23.0
National City Corp.	Ohio	5	39.1	22.7
First Chicago Corp.	Illinois	3	7.8	21.4
Key Corp.	New York	8	45.7	21.0
Bank of New York Corp., Inc.	New York	3	2.9	20.9
Bank of Boston Corp.	Massachusetts	5	30.3	19.8
Comerica, Inc.	Michigan	6	19.6	19.5
Boatmen's Bancshares, Inc.	Missouri	8	36.5	18.3

Source: John P. LaWare, Testimony before the Subcommittee on Financial Institutions Supervision, Regulation and Deposit Insurance of the Committee on Banking, Finance, and Urban Affairs, U.S. House of Representatives, June 22, 1993.

ditional banking companies represented in one or two states, people are today confronted with megacompanies like NationsBank, Wells Fargo–First Interstate, and Norwest, represented in ten or more different states, as table 1.5 shows. Not far behind were BankAmerica and Citicorp, each with bank acquisitions in nine different states, while BankOne, Key Corp., and Boatmen's Bancshares had reached into eight different states as recently as the summer of 1993. (In 1996 NationsBank moved to acquire Boatmen's Bancshares, extending the former institution's reach to 16 states, ranging from Maryland to New Mexico.) Moreover, with the federal government's longstanding prohibitions against interstate banking now being phased out, more nationwide banking companies will inevitably emerge through acquisition, branching, and merger as the twentieth century draws to a close and

Table 1.6
Number of U.S. Large Commercial Bank Mergers and Acquisitions,
1980–94*

Year	Number of Large Bank Mergers	Number of Large Interstate Mergers and Acquisitions
1980	0	0
1981	1	0
1982	2	0
1983	5	0
1984	6	0
1985	9	4
1986	9	6
1987	18	11
1988	14	7
1989	3	2
1990	6	2
1991	16	12
1992	23	15
1993	15	10
1994	15	11
Total	142	80

Note:
* Where the acquiring firm and target commercial bank are each over $1 billion in assets.

Sources: Stephen A. Rhoades, "Mergers and Acquisitions by Commercial Banks, 1980–1994," *Staff Study,* Federal Reserve Board, 4th quarter 1995; and Janet L. Yellen, Testimony before the Subcommittee on Financial Institutions and Consumer Credit, U.S. House of Representatives, October 17, 1995.

a new era begins. As table 1.6 notes, interstate bank mergers now dominate the total number of large (billion-dollar-plus) mergers occurring each year, and their representation in this wave of structural change must surely grow. What this might mean for the consumer of banking and financial services is one of the central issues pursued later in this book.

FORCES THAT HAVE BROUGHT ABOUT INTERSTATE BANKING AND OTHER RECENT CHANGES IN THE STRUCTURE OF AMERICAN BANKING

What forces have generated such sweeping changes in American banking? As with any such massive structural remaking of an industry several factors have been at work: (a) economic adversity and bank failures; (b) weaknesses in the U.S. bank regulatory system; (c) intense competition from nonbank financial-service providers; (d) the remarkable mobility of the American population, accompanied by a variety of regional demographic changes; (e) the advancing technology of service delivery; and (f) the search by American banks for greater cost savings, more loyal deposits, increased revenue synergies, and reduced earnings risk.

Economic Adversity and Bank Failures

It seems ironic that the greatest number of bank and thrift institution failures since the founding of the Federal Deposit Insurance Corporation (FDIC) took place during the longest period of continuous economic expansion in U.S. history. From 1982 until 1990 the U.S. economy enjoyed minimal unemployment and freedom from damaging recessions—a period of economic prosperity whose length and scope has never been duplicated in the United States nor in the historical record of any other nation.

Unfortunately, sustained prosperity often seems to breed contempt for prudent and careful lending practices. Moreover, the nation's overall prosperity masked serious economic problems in selected regions of the country, particularly in New England and the Southwest (especially the states of Louisiana, Oklahoma, and Texas), where the collapse of real estate and energy markets resulted in a glut of nonperforming loans that overwhelmed the capital of both large and small banking organizations. Adding to these problems over the past decade has been the collapse of the military threat from the Warsaw Pact and the Soviet Union, which has depressed banking in those parts of the U.S. (such as California and Washington) heavily dependent upon defense spending.

Anxious to find new capital in order to rescue troubled banks and thrift institutions, many states passed liberal interstate banking laws in an effort to encourage outside banking companies to enter and bring their expertise to bear upon the problems at hand. Nowhere was this more evident than in Texas, where nearly all of that state's largest banks failed or were absorbed by larger out-of-state companies. Wisely, Texas passed one of the simplest and most liberal of interstate banking laws, imposing few conditions on those interstate bankers who might be interested in entering the Lone Star State and purchasing its banks as a base for access to the huge and growing financial-service markets of the Southwest.

Weaknesses in the Regulatory System

Among the fundamental causes of consolidation and concentration in American banking were some serious errors by the U.S. regulatory community. In the 1960s and 1970s, for example, large numbers of new banks were chartered, which led to an intensification of banking competition in hundreds of local markets. Then the early 1980s brought a poorly crafted and hastily assembled attempt at deregulation of the banking and thrift industries in the form of two major federal laws: the Depository Institutions Deregulation and Monetary Control Act of 1980 and the Garn-St Germain Depository Institutions Act of 1982. These two epoch-making attempts at deregulating the depository institutions' sector took steps that significantly impacted the earnings and risk exposure of banks and their nearest competitors, the savings and loan industry.

One of these hazardous steps was the lifting of federal interest-rate ceilings on deposits, which originally had been set in place during the 1930s in an effort to prevent banks from reaching for expensive customer deposits that might erode their earnings. As these so-called Regulation Q interest-rate ceilings were phased out during the mid-1980s, banks and thrift institutions experienced an increase in both the average cost of their borrowed funds and in the volatility of their earnings, which became more sensitive to movements in market interest rates. Thus, U.S. banking's earnings stream became more risky, responding more openly to swings in credit market conditions, and some banks were unable to cope with this more volatile interest-rate environment.

Equally important was a fatal flaw in the structure of the U.S. deposit insurance system, which until 1993 levied a flat fee (insurance premium) against all banks and thrift institutions in order to provide a reservoir of government funds to backstop and protect the public's deposits. Thus, for most of the Federal Deposit Insurance Corporation's history, the riskiest banks paid the *same* insurance fee per deposit dollar as did the least risky banks, which provided a perverse incentive for those banking institutions willing to take on greater risk. More prudently managed financial firms were literally subsidizing the more risky ones, encouraging the latter to play the lottery with publicly insured deposits.

Some bankers were unable to resist the lure of being able to attract deposits at interest rates even lower than those paid by the U.S. government on Treasury bills and then reinvesting their funds in the riskiest loans possible. Moreover, Congress contributed to this so-called moral hazard problem by more than doubling deposit insurance coverage from $40,000 to $100,000 in 1980, thereby eliminating the need for carefully monitoring bank risk that many large depositors normally would have done. It was a bureaucratic system that rewarded, rather than discouraged, risk taking, and U.S. taxpayers ultimately paid the bill for these risky practices when the federal deposit insurance system was recapitalized in the early 1990s.

Competition from Nonbank Financial-Service Providers

Throughout the period since World War II, credit unions, savings and loans, mutual funds, and other nonbank financial-service providers have posed a significant challenge to banking's leadership as the premier lender, savings depository, and payments agent for households and businesses.

Gradually over the 1970s and 1980s, nonbank financial-service companies—especially credit unions, savings and loans, and other thrift institutions—received significantly expanded powers from the U.S. Congress and federal supervisory agencies to offer checking (demand) accounts—once the exclusive province of U.S. commercial banks—as well as new forms of consumer installment, credit card, home mortgage, and business loans.

Political pressure to deregulate these thrift institutions and, thereby, increase competition in the financial-services sector began with the administration of President Richard M. Nixon, founded on the belief that Americans were not receiving the full benefits of competitive pricing of financial services (particularly in access to new home loans at reasonable cost). Instead of chartering many new banks and thrifts, Congress and the president settled on a plan to lower the barriers to competition between existing banks and thrifts, so that these long-separated industries could offer many of the *same* services. This meant giving thrift institutions, who then had far fewer service powers than commercial banks, new commercial and consumer loan and deposit powers as well as access to trust services and credit cards. In contrast, commercial banks already possessed most of these new services and thus gained little (except for the lifting of federal ceilings imposed on the interest rates attached to bank deposits) from the deregulation movement of the 1980s.

Moreover, the ranks of banking's competitors were further swelled when companies like USAA began selling deposits, insurance, and other services by telephone, fax machine, and personal computer to households across the nation. At roughly the same time AT&T and other industrial and service corporations launched credit card programs as a supplement to their main business lines, while insurance companies like AIG developed a full line of financial services for large corporations—previously the mainstay of bank lending and leasing programs.

Today, as Federal Reserve Board member Edward W. Kelley, Jr. (1995, p. 3) has noted:

> Banks' nearly exclusive franchise in many areas of credit intermediation has significantly eroded. Following the lead of Merrill Lynch, retail brokers introduced close substitutes for insured demand deposit accounts. General Motors, Ford, and other automobile manufacturers offer financing that has captured a large market share of auto loans. General Electric Capital Corporation and other industrial finance companies have certain advantages, such as superior credit ratings and limited regulation, that have made them very able competitors in the commercial loan market. And, of course, the home mortgage market was completely transformed by the financial innovations of Fannie Mae and Freddie Mac. Thus, thrift institutions could become "bank-like" in their

service menus, making it harder for the public to differentiate between banks and nonbanks and forcing banks to share their market areas with more competitors.

Faced with so many new competitors, many U.S. bankers have come to view interstate expansion as the key to their future survival as viable, diversified financial-service companies.

Population Mobility and Regional Demographic Changes

A shifting population across the United States has also played a role in the banking industry's unfolding and tumultuous story of the 1980s and 1990s. As the U.S. population shifted to the South (especially to Florida, Georgia, and the Carolinas), toward the Southwest (particularly toward Texas, Arizona, and New Mexico), and to the West Coast (led by California, Nevada, Oregon, and Washington), banks in the Midwest, North Atlantic, and New England lost important customers and the revenues they would have generated from sales of their fee-based services. Thus, some of the nation's less-well-situated banks found that their capital was not growing commensurate with the risk exposures they faced. This long-range demographic trend added to the business cycle problems already developing in many areas of the United States, encouraging many bankers to seek opportunities to expand across state lines and to follow their customers into new markets. Where state laws prevented interstate expansion, banking industry groups brought pressure on state legislatures to change local banking laws and open the door to acquisitions across state boundaries.

The Advancing Technology of Service Delivery

Banking organizations seeking broader geographic markets have benefited greatly from the "information revolution" of the 1980s and 1990s. In 1980 there were less than twenty thousand ATMs dispensing cash and aiding bank customers with other routine transactions. However, by 1994 ATMs in the United States had climbed to almost 110,000. In 1980, ATMs accounted for less than $50 billion in banking transactions, but in 1994 they tallied nearly $560 billion in total transactions volume—a tenfold expansion compared to less than a doubling in the number of checks written in the United States.

And, ATM transactions were joined in the 1990s by telephone and computer network banking, which seems to offer even greater opportunities for bankers determined to reach customers scattered over different states and regions of the United States as well as those abroad. It is no mere coincidence that the emergence of full-service interstate banking has occurred at the same time as remarkable and rapid advances in communications technology have occurred, for the essence of banking is the transfer and storage of financial information that, today, can overcome most of the geographic and technical barriers that stymied earlier generations of banks and their customers.

A word of caution is in order here, however, for the number of traditional banking offices has *also* continued to grow. Despite rapid ATM growth, full-service banking offices advanced from less than forty-six thousand in 1980 to more than sixty thousand in 1994 and may continue to grow for a time alongside computer networks and automated machines to benefit those customers who do not trust or understand the new information technologies and to serve as a necessary platform for the sale of an ever expanding range of bank services, from credit and savings to retirement planning and risk management.

The Search for Cost Savings, Core Deposits, Revenue Synergies, and Reduced Earnings Risk

Coincident with all the foregoing *external forces* reshaping the banking industry were changes going on *inside* the individual banking firm that have brought closer a consolidated, national banking system. Facing strong pressures on their operating costs (especially in attracting new personnel and purchasing automated equipment), American banks have sought more efficient ways to produce and deliver their services, and more stable (core) deposits from which to build loan portfolios promising greater net yields.

American bankers have also sought new sources of revenue that complement their traditional service lines and help to stabilize revenue flows and reduce earnings risk. For many banks the answer to these needs was to enter *new* markets, first inside their home states as state law permitted and then across much wider areas encompassing whole regions of the United States as state laws were changed in the 1980s and early 1990s and as federal law was modified in the mid-1990s.

While all of these internal forces have been at work at one time or another, pushing the United States toward a truly national banking system with fewer but much larger banks, it is the *potential for cost savings* that has received the most publicity in the national news media. For example (as noted in Andersen Consulting [1994]), when BankAmerica and Security Pacific Corporation merged in April 1992, creating a combined organization with close to $190 billion in assets, management closed about one-third (nearly five hundred) of the consolidated institution's branch offices. Senior management projected that this second largest U.S. banking firm would ultimately save about $1.2 billion in operating costs as a result of consolidating its far-flung branch office system.

Similarly, when Congress was debating passage of an interstate banking bill in 1994, Hugh L. McColl, Jr., chairman of NationsBank, estimated that his bank would save close to $50 million a year by being able to convert its affiliated banks residing in ten states into simple branch offices of the lead bank, eliminating several tiers of management and duplicate staffs (as noted in Andersen Consulting [1994]). When First Interstate of Los Angeles and the First Bank System of Minneapolis announced their ill-fated merger proposal in November of 1995, the two companies projected savings of close to $500 million in reduced operating costs, stemming from the elimination of about six thousand jobs and the consolidation of data processing and other duplicated facilities. Subsequently, Wells Fargo moved in to replace the First Bank System as First Interstate's suitor and projected similarly massive cost savings and substantial job cuts.

Not only is the search for cost savings a key factor in the ongoing transformation of U.S. banking from a local to a national perspective, but there is also a powerful urge *to open up new sources of revenue and net earnings.* Interstate acquisitions, as will be seen more fully in chapter 6, have tended to focus disproportionately upon the fastest growing states and regions (such as Arizona, Florida, Georgia and the Carolinas, Illinois, and Texas)—areas that seem to offer the greatest revenue and earnings potential for the future. There has also been a significant invasion of those market areas that seem less competitive than the markets interstate banks already serve. Such market areas allow invading banks to charge higher service fees and to gather up less-expensive deposits than are usually available in more intensely competitive central city markets.

Ideally, interstate banking companies seek out those areas where markets are not only weakly competitive but also where there are well-managed banks available as targets for acquisition, so that the management of the acquiring company is *not* forced into making expensive changes from the first day following an acquisition. Moreover, as will be discussed in chapter 5, many interstate banks have benefited from an unusual feature of the financial rewards from bank mergers that does not seem to characterize most nonbank mergers. In banking, merger announcements often seem to generate abnormal (excess) returns for the stockholders of *both* acquiring and target firms, whereas in most other industries only the stockholders of the acquired firm appear to receive detectable abnormal (excess) returns. Thus, there exists a strong financial incentive on *both* sides of the bargaining table to consolidate banking firms into an industry of fewer and more dominant service providers.

REGULATORY SUPPORT FOR A MORE CONSOLIDATED BANKING SYSTEM

Supplementing all of the foregoing external and internal pressures for interstate bank expansion is the favorable attitude of most bank regulatory agencies and the U.S. Department of Justice, who see banking industry consolidation as a long-run effective solution to some of the industry's problems and weaknesses. This bias toward favoring larger, more geographically diverse banking entities is most evident in recent regulatory decisions of the Comptroller of the Currency (Administrator of National Banks) and the Federal Reserve Board. The emergence of larger, but fewer, banking companies may present regulators with fewer failing bank situations to resolve, enhance service convenience for the public, permit banks to successfully compete with less-regulated securities firms, insurance companies, and finance companies, and make U.S. banks more competitive with foreign banks in public stature, reputation, and service.

Moreover, federal antitrust policies toward mergers and acquisitions were significantly liberalized in the 1980s during the administration of President Ronald Reagan. Subsequent presidential administrations have made few significant changes in these new Department of Justice (DOJ) antitrust guidelines, with the result that the number of horizontal mergers involving industrial and service firms serving the same markets has soared. A recent simulation of the U.S. banking industry's consolidation potential under the amended DOJ guidelines by Federal Reserve Board economist Stephen A. Rhoades (1992) found ample room for further concentration of industry resources, suggesting that an eventual consolidated U.S. banking structure could reach the point where the *average* number of independent banking entities for urban and nonurban communities may be no more than *three* institutions per community.

WHERE THE STRUCTURE OF BANKING IN THE UNITED STATES IS HEADED

Clearly, banking in the United States today *is* undergoing a structural revolution. The number of independent banks is declining; large branch banking organizations are absorbing hundreds of small single-office banking firms, and bank holding companies—corporations controlling the stock of one or more banks—are expanding nationwide, accounting today for more than 90 percent of the industry's assets. True, interstate banks still represent only a minority—less than 30 percent—of industry shares but these multistate entities have more than tripled their market share since 1987.

Recently there have been many predictions of the future structure of American banking. Several analysts have predicted a future banking industry for the United States that looks very much like the banking industries of Canada, Germany, and Great Britain, where a handful of giant firms dominate the nation's banking business. For example, Paul Getman of Regional Financial Associates of West Chester, Pennsylvania, predicts there will only be four to five thousand banks by the beginning of the next century, while Andersen Consulting and the Bank Administration Institute have predicted an industry population of less than seventy-five hundred banks by the year 2000 (as noted in Andersen Consulting [1994]).

One of the most comprehensive forecasts of the future of American banking was prepared in the early 1990s by Federal Reserve Board economists Timothy Hannan and Stephen Rhoades (1992). These two banking structure specialists examined past changes in interstate laws and recent changes in the structure of the banking industry in California to extrapolate the structural makeup of U.S. banking nationwide in the year 2010. They have predicted that the number of independent banking firms will fall to 5,500 by 2010, compared to 9,908 independent banking firms in 1989. The largest one hundred banking companies would then command 87 percent of all domestic banking assets. However, Hannan and Rhoades suggest that there will still be a substantial number of smaller community-oriented banks due to "the continuing demand for conveniently located banking facilities by the great majority of consumers and small businesses." (1992, p. 797).

However, not everyone agrees with these forecasts of rapid industry shrinkage. For example, in the fall of 1995, Sage Group of Palo Alto, California—a prominent consulting firm—argued that the number of *community* (smaller and more locally focused) banks nationwide should not decline dramatically over the next several years because, as reported in their survey of the industry, close to 93 percent of existing community banks still prefer to remain independent. Sage has predicted that future merger and acquisition activity will be concentrated primarily in the nation's three hundred largest banks, leaving the remainder of the industry relatively unaffected (SNL Weekly BankFax, October 9, 1995). Moreover, in a comprehensive study of interstate banking before the Riegle-Neal Interstate Banking and Branching Efficiency Act became effective, Susan McLaughlin of the Federal Reserve Bank of New York (1995) found evidence that the passage of new banking laws does tend to accelerate industry consolidation, but that most interstate banking organizations tend to expand gradually, rather than in haste, venturing first into those states closest to their home. Thus, predictions of immediate consolidated nationwide banking and the quick absorption of thousands of independent banks *may* be drastically overblown.

Still, there is at least limited evidence that rapid structural change in American banking *is* possible. Recently Fred Furlong and Gary Zimmerman (1995) of the Federal Reserve Bank of San Francisco pointed out that recent structural changes in California's banking industry may be a signal of what is to come for the remainder of the nation once interstate branching becomes fully legalized in 1997. In California in the early 1990s the number of banks fell from 516 at the end of 1990 to just 399 in 1994—a 23 percent drop in the industry's population in just four years. Moreover, even the total number of banking offices has begun to decline in California, which recently fell from 5,555 full-service offices to 4,411 in just two years—a decline of about 20 percent. Furlong and Zimmerman predict that, while the 1980s saw a decline in the number of separate banking companies, but continuing growth in *total* banking offices, the future may well bring *both* fewer banks and fewer branch offices as banking swings from the construction of more brick and mortar facilities to greater use of computer and telephone linkages with its customers.

While deposit and payment functions in banking have long ago been automated and centralized, even the loan function may become so streamlined and automated that there will be less need in the future for human contact in banking services. For example, recent experiments by Union Planters Corporation of Tennessee and BancOne in Huntington, West Virginia, suggest that automated loan machines (ALMs) may soon become widespread, allowing customers twenty-four-hour access to credit through a computerized credit-scoring system. These machines can reach loan decisions in minutes or seconds, thus eliminating the need to meet face-to-face with a bank loan officer at a traditional bank office site. Moreover, more and more bank customers will be able to shop using the Internet and such software packages as Quicken and Money to search for the best prices available on loans, deposits, and other financial services.

When bank customers are in motion and not close to a personal computer, there will soon be electronic devices, no bigger than a wallet or purse, that make it possible to move funds out of or into your account or to retrieve useful financial information instantly. Thus, a bank customer located in Chicago may soon be able to easily secure a home mortgage loan in Kansas City, an automobile loan in Baltimore, a savings account in Boston, and a credit card from a bank in San Francisco without leaving his or her home or place of work. Customers may be able to replicate the close relationships they have enjoyed in the past with their local financial-service firms through electronic contact with service providers hundreds or thousands of miles away. Big banks through partnerships with software companies (e.g., Citicorp with Intuit or First Chicago with Microsoft) may reach into the remotest local areas. Moreover, based on California's recent experience with structural change in banking, this may happen very quickly—perhaps spanning only a few years rather than decades.[1]

While any predictions are dangerous at this stage, the following future trends in American banking seem likely over the coming decade:

1. An acceleration of the ongoing trend toward industry consolidation, with significantly fewer and much larger banking companies emerging (as noted in table 1.7). Moreover, merger partners will average much larger than in the past with fewer small acquisition targets available. As Laderman (1995) notes, many of the new services and new technologies in banking today favor larger banks (including credit enhancements, mutual funds, derivatives, and home and office finan-

Table 1.7
What Could Happen as a Result of the Expansion of Interstate Banking in the United States

- Acceleration in the industry's consolidation trend: Fewer banking alternatives with the public's deposits more concentrated in larger banking institutions.
- Fewer independently owned banks.
- Less local control over many credit decisions (which may result in less credit available to households and smaller businesses).
- Greater difficulties on the part of individual states to tax banks headquartered in other states and to regulate and examine banks that operate across multiple state lines.
- More closings of full-service branches to eliminate duplication and unprofitable locations, and greater use of limited-service offices and ATMs to replace new banking companies.
- More bank employee layoffs due to consolidation and automation of facilities.
- Greater pressure on small banks to compete or leave the industry (but the current evidence is that small banks can compete on cost).
- More banking services and added service convenience for at least sixty million people who cross state lines every day.
- Reduced government deposit insurance coverage for the individual depositor as previously separate banks are merged together into fewer separately incorporated firms.
- A more stable banking system as a result of greater service and geographic diversification.

cial-service delivery), thereby increasing the range of service output over which economies of scale can help to reduce branch costs and give the largest banking firms a substantial cost advantage.

2. Significant concentration of industry resources at state and national levels will occur, with leading banks holding increasingly larger percentages of industry assets and deposits, though local market concentration in individual cities and towns across the United States is not likely to change much for some time.

3. Large-scale closings of full-service branch banking offices is likely in the wake of many current and future domestic mergers, while automated facilities (such as automated tellers and home- and office-linked electronic devices) should continue to soar. In the 1980s and early 1990s the number of U.S. banking offices exploded to reach 65,577 by the end of 1992,

or close to 9,000 more offices than in 1984. On a per-capita basis the number of banking offices moved higher, in part, because thrift institutions were reducing their offices significantly. (For example, U.S. savings and loan offices dropped from close to twenty-six thousand to about sixteen thousand between 1988 and 1993.) However, more recently the number of U.S. full-service banking offices has leveled out (as shown in table 1.1), while automated facilities offering high-volume but limited services have climbed significantly to well over one hundred thousand units.

4. Substantial employee layoffs are likely as banking consolidation proceeds, particularly in the so-called back-office operations of banks where checks are cleared and financial data is transferred and stored. Examples include the Chemical–Manufacturers Hanover merger in 1993, where about sixty-two hundred employees were furloughed, and the Chase Manhattan–Chemical merger approved in 1995–96 that may ultimately cost close to twelve thousand industry jobs. Between 1985 and 1995, bank employment declined just over 6 percent nationwide, even as employment in the rest of the financial-services sector was rising almost 14 percent.

5. Greater pressures on small banks to compete or leave the industry. Among the most significant barriers that small banks will face in the coming decade are the need for more aggressive service innovations; the ability to accommodate customer mobility with credit, payments, and investment services; and the demanding technical requirements of tomorrow's payments and information systems.[2] However, small banks appear to be able to compete effectively on cost if they are willing to fight for their market areas and can find new investors willing to pledge sufficient capital.

6. With bigger banking firms controlling thousands of smaller local units, there may well be *less* local control over many credit and other financial-service decisions, which may result in less credit being made available for smaller businesses and households and more loans devoted to foreign and domestic corporate expansion. The public must begin to seriously consider what impact interstate banking could have on the growth and survival of small businesses in the American economy.

7. More banking services are likely to be developed as larger banks can generally command the necessary resources to develop and withstand the significant risks of service innovation.

In particular, nearly sixty million U.S. citizens who regularly cross state lines for work, shopping, or recreation should have access to not only more banking services but also to more conveniently provided services as industry consolidation proceeds.

8. A more stable American banking system may develop as a result of greater service diversification, greater geographic diversification, and a stronger industry capital base to absorb losses in the short run. Thus, there are likely to be fewer and more isolated bank failures. However, the failures that do occur should increasingly be found among the largest banking firms, creating serious problems of maintaining public confidence in the banking and financial system.

ARE BANKS DYING?

Even as interstate banks grow to take over a greater share of the industry's resources, there is some evidence that the American banking industry as a whole is losing ground to nonbank financial-service competitors. The proportion of total assets held by banks relative to all financial institutions seems to point toward a substantial *decline* in banking's proportion of the U.S. financial sector's total resources, while mutual funds, pension plans, and even credit unions continue to capture a rising share of financial transactions and assets. Some observers believe the American banking industry is *dying*, to be replaced eventually by better diversified, more security-oriented firms who face fewer regulations. In this view even the rise in interstate banking cannot save American banks from their ultimate destiny to play a smaller and smaller role in financial affairs.

While the "banking is dying" theory seems plausible to many observers today, there are good reasons to seek a "second opinion" on the industry's prognosis. For one thing a growing proportion of banking activity is no longer recorded on bank balance sheets. This includes such activities as selling and managing mutual funds, underwriting security offerings for corporate customers, and trading in financial futures and options. When adjustments are made for these so-called off-balance-sheet activities, it is not clear at all that banking's share of the economy has gone down. Indeed, by some more inclusive measures (such as the industry's share of gross domestic product and total sales), banks may have held their own relative to most other financial-service firms.

While banking may not be dying, it is certainly becoming different from the industry recognized by earlier generations. It is, more than ever, an industry focused upon *information*—gathering, processing, and evaluating data for itself and the public it serves. Buffeted by the rapidly shifting character and possibilities of the information age, banking must become more efficient, more service responsive, and more focused on the central roles so that it can profitably perform in tomorrow's economy. Banking as most people know it need not die, but it must certainly *change* in order to survive, as must the people who manage and direct its talent and resources. Interstate expansion may help to insure the banking industry's long-run survival and arrest its recent loss of market share to nonbank financial firms provided that interstate companies, through their service policies and production efficiencies, are better able to deliver those services most in public demand at lowest cost. Whether such a favorable outcome will occur as interstate banking spreads across the United States and comes to dominate the assets and deposits held by all American banks is an open question very much in need of future research.

NOTES

1. Of course, what these forecasters may have forgotten is the opportunities recent industry consolidation may have created for *new* banks. Between 1980 and 1995 about thirty-two hundred new banks were launched, roughly half the number absorbed by merger over the same period (as illustrated in table 1.3). Far from disappearing, community banks have been successful in focusing upon unique niches—personalized service for families, small businesses, and professionals—and these special customer niches may be difficult and costly for larger, more distant banks to duplicate qualitatively.

2. For example, one relatively small bank holding company in the author's home town sold out to a leading midwestern holding company simply because it couldn't keep abreast of growing check processing burdens and new industry and government standards for payments services.

CHAPTER 2

Background to Interstate Banking: Early Federal and State Interstate Banking Laws

For much of the eighteenth and nineteenth centuries, where American banks were located and how far they could go in branching and entering new markets was *not* an issue for debate. Until the 1860s, banks in the United States were generally allowed free reign in setting up, moving, or closing their branch offices. States that did impose restrictions on banks creating branch offices were primarily motivated by a desire to stop poorly managed banks from overissuing currency, contributing to a loss of public confidence in government and the banking system.

At that time banking firms made loans to their customers by issuing their own bank notes that circulated as currency but could be redeemed for gold and silver bullion upon public demand. This ever present threat of being able to convert paper bank notes into gold and silver coinage compelled banks to be more prudent in their lending activities; otherwise, overlending could lead the public to lose confidence in a particular bank and demand payment in gold or silver, thereby exhausting the bank's precious metal reserves. Many poorly managed banks set up branch offices ("redemption centers") in remote locations in an effort to frustrate the public's efforts to convert paper notes into a form of money more stable in value. Thus, the purpose of many of the early bank branch offices was *not* convenience for the public but to discourage currency conversions and protect bank profits.

Still, a few states outlawed branching even in the nineteenth century. When the U.S. Congress made its first foray into banking by chartering the

Bank of the United States in order to facilitate government transactions and protect the integrity of the dollar, no restrictions were imposed on that bank's territorial expansion, and branch offices were set up in several states. However, these branches were really more like subsidiary companies of the Bank of the United States rather than being subservient units of a highly integrated and centralized banking organization. As Sommer (1993) has observed, public objections to the rechartering of the Bank of the United States, which ultimately led to its demise, centered not on that bank's branching activities across state lines but upon its constitutionality, its stock subscription policies, and its apparent bias toward eastern business interests as opposed to the credit-starved newly developing areas of the nation.

For their part, the individual state governments generally were silent on the branching issue, largely because most banks were rooted in a single community and there was little need for distant branch offices. However, by the latter part of the nineteenth century, technological advances and an increasingly mobile population brought many smaller community banks into competition with established city banks. State legislators began to respond to pleas from local bankers to erect legislated barriers to the entry of outside competition. As a result, complicated state laws were soon passed, severely restricting branch office expansion. Some states, such as Colorado, Texas, and Oklahoma, prohibited all branching activity, while others (such as Michigan and New York) limited branching to home-office cities, counties, or special districts.

EARLY FEDERAL GOVERNMENT INVOLVEMENT IN AMERICAN BANKING

From the earliest days of the American experience, there has been controversy over what role the federal government of the United States should be allowed to play within the nation's banking system. The first incorporated bank in the United States, the Bank of North America, was incorporated by the Continental Congress in Philadelphia in December 1781 and played a significant role in helping the nation gain its independence from Europe. However, a year later the State of Pennsylvania issued a state charter for this bank, in part due to an ongoing controversy as to whether or not the federal government could legally award bank charters. The U.S. Constitution, for example, made no mention of federal bank chartering powers. It simply grants Congress the power to coin money and regulate its value. Broadly construed, this could (and eventually did) open the door to both federal chartering of banks and the creation of a central bank—the Federal Reserve System.

The debate over whether Congress or some other branch of the federal government had the power to create new private banks continued during the era of the First Bank of the United States, which, thanks to strong lobbying by Alexander Hamilton, the U.S. Treasury Secretary, received its initial federal charter in 1791. This action was vehemently opposed by forces in Congress who believed the central government should be kept weaker than the governments of the individual states and by a variety of private groups—mainly bankers representing state-chartered banks—which feared First Bank's competition. Ultimately, First Bank's charter was allowed to expire in 1811 at the conclusion of its initial twenty-year term.

The Second Bank of the United States was chartered by Congress in 1816 to bring some measure of stability to the early U.S. banking system and stop bank runs by worried depositors. Many depositors feared the loss of their money due to an economic recession and the War of 1812 with Great Britain, which some feared the U.S. might lose. An attempt by the states to tax the Second Bank out of existence soon led to a landmark U.S. Supreme Court decision by Chief Justice John Marshall. In the famous *McCulloch v. Maryland* case in 1819 (17 U.S. 316) Justice Marshall ruled that a state could not tax a bank chartered by the federal government—a dictum that seemed to support the notion that the federal government *did* have the power to create federally chartered (national) banks. Nevertheless, reflecting the bitter and, at times, irrational opposition of President Andrew Jackson and others, the Second Bank's charter was not renewed in 1832, and it eventually closed, giving way to a state-dominated "free banking" era in the United States, where bank charters were not required as a condition for starting a bank. Instead, new banks could be set up merely by pledging sufficient capital and conforming to the specific dictates of state law.

Few banks in the United States then had branch offices except in the South and in portions of the Midwest. Banks along the East Coast, especially in the New England and Middle Atlantic regions, were mainly wholesale banks—servicing businesses—and therefore had little reason to establish branches. The Civil War brought an end to most of the Confederacy's branching banks in the 1860s, however. Thus, when the first national banks were chartered by the federal government under the National Bank Act of 1863–64, no branches appeared at most of these banks because of lack of public demand.

THE NATIONAL BANK ACT OF 1863–64

The landmark National Bank Act of 1863–64 ushered in the current era of federal government involvement in America's banking industry. This law created the Office of the Comptroller of the Currency (OCC)—the oldest federal bank regulatory agency—to issue certificates of association in order to form new *national banks*, which throughout their corporate lifetimes would be supervised and regulated by the OCC. At one stroke in the National Bank Act, Congress created a *dual banking system*, with both the individual states and the federal government chartering, supervising, and

Table 2.1
The Dual Banking System of Regulation in the United States

FEDERAL REGULATORY AUTHORITIES

Comptroller of the Currency (OCC)
Supervises and examines national banks that are chartered by the Comptroller of the Currency's Office in Washington, D.C., a division of the United States Treasury Department. The Comptroller must approve any merger or acquisition involving national banks and declare a national bank insolvent before its assets can be purchased or liquidated.

Federal Reserve System (FRS)
Supervises member banks of the Federal Reserve System (which include national banks), but usually examines only state-chartered banks that have elected to join the Federal Reserve System. The formation and the acquisitions of bank holding companies must be approved by the Federal Reserve Board in Washington, D.C., which also monitors and enforces federal law against all foreign banks operating inside the United States and the foreign ventures of American banks.

Federal Deposit Insurance Corporation (FDIC)
Supervises all federally insured banks that have qualified for FDIC insurance coverage of their deposits, but usually examines only state-chartered banks not members of the Federal Reserve System. The FDIC prepares standards for the prudent management of all federally insured banks in an effort to protect federal insurance reserves.

STATE BANKING AUTHORITIES

State banking boards or commissions supervise and examine all banks chartered by the state where each bank is headquartered and may reserve the power to approve or disapprove of any mergers or acquisitions involving state-chartered banks. When a state bank fails, it must be declared insolvent by the state's banking board or commission and may then be turned over to the FDIC acting as receiver for the disposition of the failed bank's assets and deposits.

---

regulating banks (see table 2.1 for an overview of the current dual banking system of regulation in the United States).

Unfortunately, Congress chose not to be specific about whether national banks had branching powers nor were the services these banks could offer really spelled out. For example, Section 8 (13 Stat. 99) of the Act states:

> [A national bank] may . . . exercise under this act all such incidental powers as shall be necessary to carry on the business of banking by discounting and negotiating promissory notes, drafts, bills of exchange, and other evidences of debt; by receiving de-

posits; by buying and selling exchange, coin, and bullion; by loaning money on personal security; by obtaining, issuing, and circulating notes according to provisions of this act.

With such vagueness in the new law's provisions, the branching and service powers of federally chartered banks were left to the Comptroller of the Currency and the courts to interpret.

As economist Larry Mote (1974) has observed, every Comptroller of the Currency from Freeman Clarke in 1865 to D. R. Crissinger in 1922 held that national banks could *not* operate from more than one location. But any state banks that operated branches were permitted to continue to operate those branches if they became national banks under the Comptroller's authority. And, in 1922 Comptroller Daniel Crissinger approved the opening of limited-service facilities by national banks provided these facilities were confined to the banks' home-office communities and situated inside states that permitted some form of branch banking.

With the passage of the National Bank Act Congress hoped to destroy the state chartering of banks and persuade state banks to apply for federal charters. However, while many state banks took the hint and signed up for national certificates, others fought back and expanded their market areas. Congress replied by taxing the notes issued by state banks that then circulated as currency. Because many of these notes were overissued and circulated at sharply discounted prices, Congress saw the act of forcing state banks into the federal system as a way to restore public confidence in the nation's circulating currency. National banks would also be called upon to help support the prosecution of the Civil War, as federally chartered banks were compelled to buy government bonds to back any bank notes they issued. Unfortunately for Congress's grand strategy to reconfigure the nation's banking system, a new monetary asset—demand deposits—soon became popular with the public. These new checkable accounts allowed banks to make loans simply by creating deposits rather than by issuing bank notes. Before long, the growth of the state bank system was outstripping the federal banking system's growth.

However, as a practical matter, most banks saw little need to branch until later in the nineteenth and early twentieth centuries, when the U.S. population became more mobile and large numbers of people began to gravitate toward the larger cities. The rise of the automobile (including truck and bus traffic) drastically altered the commuting habits of millions of Americans and placed greater pressure on banks to conform to the financial-service needs of a more geographically diverse and highly mobile population. Still, government authorities generally refused to be flexible on bankers' branching powers.

THE McFADDEN-PEPPER ACT

The branching issue remained a matter of uncertainty into the early years of the twentieth century. Household (or retail) deposits were growing in significance as a source of bank funds, and many banks, especially the largest, began to pressure state legislatures and the federal government for permission to branch. Due to communications problems, however, most branch offices in this era were in the same city as a bank's head office facility. As communication links improved, however, larger banks expressed a desire for branch systems covering neighboring counties and whole states. Congressional debate ultimately led to passage of the McFadden-Pepper Act. This 1927 law permitted national banks to set up branch offices in their home-office cities provided state-chartered banks possessed similar branching powers.

The McFadden-Pepper Act required a national bank's certificate of association (a necessary document that had to precede each national bank's opening for business) to state "the place where its operations of discount and deposit are to be carried on, designating the state, territory, or district, and the particular county, city, town, or village" (Revised Statutes § 5134). Because the law did not say "places," but only "place" where a national bank would conduct its operations, federal law was widely interpreted to *outlaw* national bank branching—a position that was upheld by the U.S. Supreme Court in the First National Bank in St. Louis case (263 U.S. 640, 657), decided in 1924. Because some states had already voted to allow their state-chartered depositories to branch, some national banks began leaving the national banking system in order to gain branching powers. Therefore, the McFadden-Pepper Act was really a stop-gap measure aimed at slowing this exodus from the national system by granting national banks parallel branching powers to those of state-chartered banks. Implicit in McFadden-Pepper, then, was a fundamental desire in Congress to protect and preserve the dual banking system—a common theme in American banking law and regulation that has lasted for well over a century. Yet, as we will see, passage of interstate banking legislation in the 1990s represented, in many ways, a decisive turn *away* from the dual banking system.

Interestingly enough, subsequent court rulings further restricted national bank branching powers when these appeared to be in conflict with the states by striking down bankers' attempts to do an "end run" around the McFadden-Pepper Act by setting up special kinds of "branches." For example, a Florida bank, First National Bank in Plant City, tried to operate an armored car as a mobile branch to allow customers to come in and cash checks and receive deposits. In 1967 the U.S. Supreme Court held that this "limited branch" mobile service unit still represented a branch office and, therefore, was in violation of McFadden-Pepper (as reported in 274 F. Supp. 449 [1967]). The court reasoned that the armored car branch offered at least one banking service that a full-service bank office is permitted to provide and, therefore, seemed to meet the broadest federal definition of a bank branch. Surprisingly, the Supreme Court held that the federal government, not necessarily the states, had the power to *define* the nature of a bank branch (at least for national banks). Thus, while the states held most of the trump cards in controlling the expansion of U.S. banks across the countryside via branches, the federal government could retain the right to decide what activities or functions constituted a full-fledged branch office.

Subsequently, challenges were made in the courts against other forms of branch banking. For example, if a national bank operated a drive-in window or an ATM remote from its main office, did this constitute branching in violation of the McFadden-Pepper Act? Mixed rulings appeared (for example, *North Davis Bank v. First National Bank of Layton*, 457 F. 2d 820 [10th Cir. 1972]), but the courts generally allowed drive-in facilities where there appeared to be no significant competitive advantage for one bank over another or where competitors had the legal and economic capacity to set up drive-in facilities as well. However, ATMs were generally considered to be branches and, therefore, contrary to McFadden-Pepper (as noted, for example, in *Colorado v. First National Bank of Fort Collins*, 540 F. 2d 497 [10th Cir. 1976]), unless a bank could find a way to offer services through automated machines owned by someone else.

Bankers ran into similar legal restrictions when opening so-called loan production offices to advertise their services, unless they could show that these offices were not actually making loan decisions and dispensing loanable funds to customers. At about the same time a number of bank holding companies attempted to use their affiliated banks as *agents* in taking deposits and accepting loan payments or in dispensing cash and loan proceeds to customers on behalf of other banks belonging to the same holding company. (See, for example, *Independent Bankers Association of America v. Heimann*, 627 F. 2d 486 [1980].) Moreover, even when national banks attempted to skirt around their traditional services—taking deposits, cashing checks, or extending credit—to offer peripheral services (for example, trust services or annuities), many courts moved again to block these forays by declaring the offices through which peripheral services were sold to be bank branches and, therefore, in technical violation of the provisions of the McFadden-Pepper Act.

The Comptroller of the Currency has been considered in modern times to be among the most liberal of the bank regulatory agencies, following decades of often extreme conservatism in the early years of the Comptroller's history. This more liberal approach has been especially evident in not only the new services (such as annuities, mutual funds, or security brokerage services) the Comptroller has sanctioned but also in the Comptroller's efforts to gradually confine in narrower and narrower limits the concept of what *is* a "branch office."

Over time (particularly in the 1980s and 1990s) more and more service functions were allowed by the Comptroller to be offered through special offices or systems of offices, provided the actual approval of loans or the awarding of loanable funds into accounts of borrowers were not carried out at the same sites as where loan applications were received. Lock box and messenger services—two devices national banks tried to offer to supply greater customer convenience and speed—were generally approved by the Comptroller within certain limits that ensured the offering national banks were not gaining a significant competitive advantage over other depository institutions (particularly over banks licensed by the states). When many national banks launched joint ventures with other financial institutions in which the banks involved did not actually own or control the offices where customer accounts were advertised and taken in, the Comptroller was usually quick to approve these particular transactions.

Overall, prior to the passage of the Riegle-Neal Interstate Banking Act it has seemed that, to be called branches at the federal level, a bank office must provide traditional banking services, be under the bank's control, and represent a competitive edge for the bank involved in pulling in new customers from other banks operating in the same market area. If applicant banks could show that at least *some* of these requirements were not met, then the bank involved would probably be able to proceed with its proposed new facility. Perhaps more telling for the future, given recent advances in the technology of service delivery, the Comptroller in July of 1993 ruled that a telemarketing facility that solicits accounts by telephone and is used to evaluate loan applications is *not* a branch bank office and, therefore, is not subject to federal antibranching laws.

Unfortunately, McFadden-Pepper did not go far enough in the minds of some national bankers because it limited national bank branching to the home office city if state law also allowed citywide branching for state-chartered banks. New legislation would eventually be needed to broaden national bank branching powers outward to the borders of a state, provided state law expressly permitted state-chartered banks to also branch statewide. Nevertheless, in its day McFadden-Pepper was aimed at liberalizing banking laws to encourage greater competition between federal and state-chartered banks rather than erecting new barriers to the cleansing force of competition.

The clear message of McFadden-Pepper was that state law was allowed to precede federal law in determining whether all banks—national and state—possessed branching authority in local areas. And, in the wake of McFadden-Pepper's enactment, six states passed legislation explicitly outlawing branch banking. Moreover, the McFadden-Pepper Act expressly prohibited interstate branching by member banks of the Federal Reserve System, while state laws were allowed to govern whether nonmember banks could branch across state lines. Most states remained silent on the issue of permitting interstate banking. Because each state's express written approval for interstate expansion was required, this effectively slammed the door on interstate full-service banking through local offices for more than half a century until the 1980s arrived.

THE GLASS-STEAGALL ACT

Six years after passage of the McFadden Act, Congress responded to the cataclysmic economic and financial problems of the Great Depression by passing the Glass-Steagall (National Banking) Act in 1933. Glass-Steagall extended the McFadden-Pepper Act's concept of allowing federally chartered (national) banks to branch in the same geographical areas as state-chartered banks. Thus, if state-chartered banks were granted no branching powers by their home states, national banks headquartered in those states could not branch either. On the other hand, if state-chartered banks could branch statewide, then national banks must be granted the same privilege under the terms of the Glass-Steagall Act. Soon, more than half the states restricted or prohibited banks from setting up branch offices. None voted to permit interstate expansion via the establishment of full-service branch offices.

These restrictions on bank branching may have worsened the Great Depression of the 1930s, when more than nine thousand American banks failed. Whereas the United States could count nearly thirty thousand banks in 1920, the industry's population sank to only about fifteen thousand in 1940. Critics of antibranching rules pointed out that if banks had been allowed to branch freely, they would not have been so completely dependent on the economic fortunes of a single community. When the local community collapsed economically, so did the bank whose revenues and profits depended on the success or failure of those local business firms that accounted for most of a community bank's loan portfolio and for the majority of its deposits. Moreover, when local businesses were forced to cut their payrolls, unemployed workers could no longer pay off their loans, and many left town, taking their deposits with them. Banks began to contract in size, and thousands failed as huge earnings losses absorbed their limited capital. Hardest hit of all were hundreds of rural communities that lost their only local bank.

The banking crisis of the 1930s led to a crumbling of at least some public resistance to American banks' branching. Sensing a moment of opportunity, larger money-center banks pushed for greater branching powers. Bankers favoring branching expressed the belief that a branch office could be run at substantially less cost and on a significantly smaller scale than a single-office bank and that a multiple-branch system tying together multiple communities would be far more stable (as Chapman and Westerfield [1942] observed). As already noted, the Glass-Steagall Act granted broader statewide branching authority to national banks but only if the individual states approved of this expanded authority. However, many states were persuaded by smaller banks *not* to grant broader branching powers on the grounds that small banks would be overwhelmed by "excessive competition" and local consumers would then be confronted with banking "monopolies." A major concern of the time, which has persisted to this day, was that large branch banks would drain away local savings in order to make investments in the largest cities, reducing local credit availability and impoverishing smaller communities.

Faced with conflicting public opinion on the issue, Congress voted to limit intrastate branching powers to no more than what the states granted to their own banks. Moreover, to win this political concession of broader branching powers, the nation's leading money-center banks were compelled to give up one of their most profitable services—investment banking (especially the underwriting of new corporate stocks and bonds). The Glass-Steagall Act legally separated commercial banking from investment banking, creating two distinct industries served by different firms.

One important additional reason why Congress was unwilling to go further in liberalizing U.S. banks' authority to branch, both within and across state lines, even in the face of the massive banking debacle of the Great Depression, was the belief that safety and stability could be brought to the nation's banking industry by simpler means. For example, it was far easier, at least in the eyes of the public, to simply prohibit banks from holding corporate stock and to outlaw banks' trading in corporate shares in order to promote bank safety. Moreover, Congress created the Federal Deposit Insurance Corporation in 1933 to protect small deposits (up to $2,500). This new insurance fund snapped the link in the public's mind between the failure of one bank and the vulnerability of other banks serving the same community and, thus, made large-scale bank "runs" largely a relic of history. After taking these major steps to restore public confidence in the American banking system, the U.S. Congress saw little need to further open the controversial Pandora's box of branch banking.

Nevertheless, as table 2.2 shows, American banks operated nearly three thousand branch offices (not counting their main or home offices) in 1934, a year after the Glass-Steagall Act was passed. After World War II, the number of branch facilities literally exploded, more than doubling during the 1950s. By the early 1960s the number of branches had climbed to a greater count than the number of main or home offices. By 1970 the industry operated more than twenty-one thousand branches and, in 1985, more than doubled that figure when the number of branches climbed over forty-three thousand. Part of the reason for this surge was a vote by twenty-two states to reduce their restrictions against branching during the 1980s. Of the states that allowed no branching at the end of 1982 all but Iowa had voted to allow at least limited branching by 1993. Finally, in 1994, the year the

Table 2.2
Growth in U.S. Banking Offices, Assets, and Income, 1934–95
(selected years)

Years	Main Offices of U.S. Insured Banks	Branch Offices of U.S. Insured Banks	Total Banking Offices	Total Assets (in Billions of Dollars)	Net After-Tax Income (in Billions of Dollars)
1934	14,146	1,985	17,131	46	(0.4)
1940	13,442	3,489	16,931	71	0.4
1946	13,359	3,926	17,287	147	0.9
1952	13,439	5,486	18,925	187	1.1
1958	13,124	8,957	22,081	237	2.1
1964	13,493	14,703	28,196	345	2.6
1970	13,511	21,810	35,321	570	4.8
1976	14,411	31,322	45,733	1,182	7.8
1982	14,451	39,784	54,235	2,194	14.8
1988	13,137	46,619	59,756	3,131	24.8
1994	10,450	55,144	65,594	4,011	44.7
1995	10,323	56,978	67,301	4,313	48.8

Notes:
Beginning in 1982 remote service facilities (ATMs) were not included in the branch office count. Banks with foreign offices reported their income on a consolidated basis after 1975. Asset totals are as of year-end.

Source: Federal Deposit Insurance Corporation, *Statistics on Banking*, Washington, D.C., 1994; 1995 figures are preliminary from the Federal Reserve Board, *Annual Report, 1995*, and Federal Deposit Insurance Corporation, *The FDIC Quarterly Banking Profile*, 1st quarter 1996.

Riegle-Neal Interstate Banking and Branching Efficiency Act was passed, total branch offices of U.S. insured banks exceeded fifty-five thousand, or about five times the number of FDIC-insured bank depositories. Not surprisingly, as table 2.2 also shows, the U.S. banking industry's assets and income expanded almost step for step with its growth in office facilities serving the public.

THE BANK HOLDING COMPANY ACT AND ITS SUBSEQUENT AMENDMENTS

Expansion-minded bankers were thus blocked from entering distant new markets by both state antibranching laws and federal inaction and sought other legal loopholes that might still permit them to follow their increasingly mobile customers with new, more conveniently located facilities. Bank holding companies—corporations that held the stock of one or more banks—gained rapidly in popularity among larger banking firms due to certain tax and borrowing advantages that they possessed.

For example, a holding company could use the losses incurred by one of the bank or nonbank businesses that it controlled to offset the profits achieved by other businesses belonging to the same company, thereby lowering its overall tax liability. Similarly, a holding company could gain additional borrowing capacity through the use of "double leveraging." Each affiliated firm belonging to the holding company could borrow based upon the strength in its own assets, and the holding company itself could also borrow against the strength of its assets, which included the stock of its affiliated firms.

In the United States, bank holding companies became a significant force in the industry in the 1920s and 1930s, often welding together in one corporate confederation large groups of separately incorporated banks serving multiple cities. These institutions spread across state lines, led by such aggressive organizations as California-based First Interstate Banks. Pressured by both small banks, who feared the market power of these interstate giants, and several large money-center banks, which feared the loss of revenue from correspondent services they were selling to smaller banks as the holding companies grew, Congress responded with passage of the Bank Holding Company Act in 1956 and the Douglas Amendment to that law a year later. These new federal rules compelled holding companies controlling two or more banks to register with the Federal Reserve Board and allowed controlling interstate bank acquisitions by bank holding companies only if the states whose banks were to be acquired specifically granted permission.

When the Bank Holding Company was passed in 1956, no state permitted outside entry by holding companies. Several existing interstate companies were grandfathered by the new law, however, which allowed these grandfathered companies to hold onto their existing interstate affiliates but restricted their ability to make further bank acquisitions without express state authorization. Most of the grandfathered interstate holding companies were quite small. The four biggest (as measured by total deposits) claimed just over 85 percent of all deposits then held by interstate holding-company banks. Gradually the grandfathered companies disappeared, some converting to one-bank companies that were not covered by the 1956 law, while others merged, so that, eventually, only seven grandfathered interstate firms remained.

A small exception to the prohibition against interstate expansion was granted under the terms of the Douglas Amendment, sponsored by Senator Paul Douglas of Illinois. Bank holding companies were permitted to acquire and hold *less than 5 percent* of the outstanding ownership shares of a bank in another state without needing state permission. However, acquisition of more than 5 percent of the stock of a bank situated in another state required the permission of the state to be entered under the terms of the Douglas Amendment. Later, in 1970, further amendments to the Bank Holding Company Act stipulated that even bank holding companies controlling only *one* bank were brought under the tight federal restrictions against acquiring banking offices across state lines. Thus, following passage of the Bank Holding Company Act and its subsequent amendments, branching within their home states remained the principal full-service growth option for the vast majority of American banks. (See table 2.3 for a brief summary of key federal laws affecting the historical expansion of U.S. banking.)

STATE LAWS OF THE 1970S, 1980S, AND 1990S

As the 1970s began, no states permitted cross-border full-service banking ventures, except for the handful of bank branches and banking companies grandfathered by the McFadden-Pepper and Glass-Steagall Acts and by the Bank Holding Company Act and its subsequent amendments. Without question, any U.S. bank could contact customers in states other than its home state in order to sell selected services to these out-of-state customers. Moreover, bank holding companies could start or acquire *nonbank* business ventures anywhere in the United States provided these nonbank firms offered services that were "closely related to banking," such as a finance company, mortgage banking unit, or leasing company. But no U.S. bank could set up office facilities in another state in order to accept deposits, make direct loans, or provide the hundreds of other interrelated services traditionally associated with banking.

Then during the late 1970s the State of Maine, in an effort to attract outside capital in order to promote its own economic development, voted to allow full-service bank entry under the terms of the Douglas Amendment to the Bank Holding Company Act. Thus, bank holding companies from outside Maine could enter and purchase controlling interest in that state's banks subject to certain conditions. The most important condition was the requirement that the state whose banking companies wished to enter Maine must grant similar entry privileges to Maine's banks. This later "reciprocity" provision proved to be a significant stumbling block for several years because no other state was willing to pass the necessary enabling legislation.

Beginning in the early 1980s, however, the floodgates of the legal dam that had held back interstate expansion for decades began to split open. Alaska, Massachusetts, and New York passed interstate entry laws that took effect in 1982. Delaware and South Dakota voted to allow the credit card and insurance operations of out-of-state banks to set up shop inside their territories and sell these services nationwide. Soon, state after state responded to pleas from local banks and consumer groups to level the competitive playing field and opened their doors to interstate expansion. By the early 1990s, forty-nine of the fifty states (excepting Hawaii) had passed some

Table 2.3
Key U.S. Banking Laws that Have Shaped the Structure of the American Banking Industry

---

National Bank Acts of 1863–64
Created an office (the Comptroller of the Currency) to charter new national banks and supervise their operations and financial condition. The law, however, mentioned no national bank branching powers, leaving the issue to legal and regulatory interpretation.

McFadden-Pepper Act of 1927
Allowed national banks chartered by the Comptroller of the Currency to branch within their home-office cities if banks chartered by the states possessed similar branching powers.

Glass-Steagall (National Banking) Act of 1933
Permitted national banks to branch anywhere within a state if state-chartered banks had been granted parallel branching privileges; branching across state lines was prohibited unless a state gave express permission to do so.

Bank Holding Company Act of 1956 and its subsequent amendments
Required stock-holding companies that held shares in banks to register with the Federal Reserve Board and gain approval for any additional bank stock acquisitions. Acquisition of controlling interest of out-of-state banks required the express approval of the states involved as well as the sanction of the Federal Reserve Board. Bank holding companies could acquire or start nonbank business firms across state lines but only if these nonbank businesses offered services "closely related to banking."

Bank Merger Act of 1960 and its amendments
Merger transactions involving federally supervised banks must have the approval of their principal federal supervisor (which is the Comptroller of the Currency for national banks; the Federal Reserve for state-chartered member banks; and the FDIC for state-chartered nonmember banks). Mergers with substantially adverse effects on competition will not generally be approved unless there are offsetting public benefits (such as the rescue of a failing bank).

Garn-St Germain Depository Institutions Act of 1982
A large failing bank or thrift institution (with $500 million or more in total assets) may be merged with a banking organization headquartered in another state provided there is no viable merger alternative within the home state of the failing institution.

---

form of interstate banking statute, allowing out-of-state entry under a wide variety of entry conditions. (Hawaii eventually voted to allow out-of-state entry during the first quarter of 1995.) Among the key motives for these liberating state laws were *economic factors* (especially a desire to bring in new capital and for banks to reach efficient size, as well as to open up attractive markets in new areas), *demographic factors* (such as greater customer mobility), *financial factors* (such as a desire of some bankers to increase the demand for their bank's stock), and *competitive factors* (such as when banks in neighboring states received more lenient expansion rules and when competing nonbank financial-service firms, such as thrift institutions and investment companies, found ways to cross state lines).

By early 1993 all states except Hawaii permitted some version of full-service interstate bank expansion, and eight states actually allowed cross-border branching (though only for state-chartered banks that were mostly too small to take advantage of these new cross-border opportunities), as tables 2.4 and 2.5 show. However, a substantial portion of the states restricted entry to bank holding companies from their own geographic area of the nation—known as *regional reciprocity* laws. Thus, some states (such as Massachusetts and North Carolina) allowed banking companies to enter only if they originated from the surrounding region of the nation. Gradually, however, as states realized there would be no great rush of outside banks into their home territories because of capital shortages and other economic factors, regional reciprocity statutes gave way to national reciprocity laws that allowed entry from *any* other state in the union provided that reciprocal privileges were granted to the entered state's banks.

For some states, though, even this liberalizing step to national reciprocity was not enough. This group, led by Texas, moved proactively to open their borders to any banking company in the nation without reciprocity required. Most of these states were struggling economically due to declining oil and gas prices and a crisis in the mortgage market as commercial and residential property values plummeted. Allowing interstate banking companies to enter appeared to be a step toward bringing in new capital and new jobs as well as rescuing local banks headed toward failure.

Left to themselves, the states created a bewildering patchwork of interstate banking rules with various restrictions on who could enter their territory and under what conditions. Most troubling were the remaining regional reciprocity requirements, which served to divide the nation into isolated banking regions (such as the New England area, the southeastern states, and the Rocky Mountain region) and, thereby, protect the leadership positions of dominant regional banks. As will be seen in the next chapter, one of the most important contributions made by passage of the Riegle-Neal Interstate Banking Law of 1994 was to strike down these regional reciprocity rules and allow bank holding companies to expand nationwide.

Neither the state banking laws of the 1980s and early 1990s nor the federal Riegle-Neal Interstate Banking Act of 1994 were easy to pass. There was strong opposition to these innovations in banking law at almost every turn. A major cause of delay and opposition was the desire of smaller banks to be protected from the prospect of "monopoly power" that might drive smaller banking firms out of business. At the extreme, if interstate banking might lead to the dominance of only a handful of large banks (similar to

Table 2.4
Types of Interstate Banking Laws in the United States (as of June 1, 1993)

Entry from any other States Allowed if Reciprocal Permission to Enter is Granted to Banks Headquartered in the State Entered (National Reciprocity)	Entry from any other State Allowed Without a Requirement That Reciprocal Entry Privileges Be Granted to Banks in the State Entered (National, No Reciprocity)	Entry from any State in the Same Region Allowed if Reciprocity is Granted to Banks Headquartered in the State Entered (Regional Reciprocity)	Entry from Other States Allowed Under Special Circumstances[2]	Entry from Out of State Still Not Permitted	States Limiting the Share of Total Deposits That Outside Banking Organizations Can Hold (Limit in percent of total bank or total bank and thrift deposits statewide that can be held by interstate banking organizations is Shown in Parentheses)[1]
California	Alaska	Alabama	Oklahoma	Hawaii	Arkansas (25%)
Connecticut	Arizona	Arkansas			Colorado (25%)
Delaware	Colorado	District of			Iowa (10%)
Illinois	Idaho	Columbia			Kansas (12%)
Indiana	Maine	Florida[3]			Kentucky (15%)
Kentucky	Nevada	Georgia			Massachusetts (15%)
Louisiana	New	Iowa			Minnesota (30%)
Massachusetts	Hampshire	Kansas			Mississippi (19%)
Michigan	New Mexico	Maryland			Montana (18%)
Nebraska	Oregon	Minnesota			Nebraska (14%)
New Jersey	Texas	Mississippi			New Hampshire (20%)
New York	Utah	Missouri			North Dakota (19%)
North Dakota	Wyoming	Montana			Ohio (20%)
Ohio		North Carolina			Oklahoma (11%)
Pennsylvania		South Carolina			Tennessee (16.5%)
Rhode Island		Virginia			Texas (25%)
South Dakota		Wisconsin			West Virginia (20%)
Tennessee					
Vermont					
Washington					
West Virginia					

Notes:

[1] All states listed in this column include total statewide bank deposits in figuring the maximum share of deposits that an interstate acquirer is allowed to hold. Certain states (Colorado, Iowa, Kentucky, Minnesota, Mississippi, Montana, Nebraska, New Hampshire, North Dakota, Ohio, Oklahoma, Tennessee, and West Virginia) also include thrift (savings and loan and savings bank) deposits. A few of the states (including Colorado, Iowa, Kentucky, Minnesota, Mississippi, Montana, New Hampshire, North Dakota, Oklahoma, Tennessee, and West Virginia) also include credit union deposits in the permissible statewide share.

[2] National entry from states offering reciprocal entry privileges or the entering organization must wait four years to expand its share.

[3] Florida has recently passed a nationwide banking bill.

Sources: Financial Structure Section of the Board of Governors of the Reserve System, and Donald T. Savage, "Interstate Branching: A Status Report," *Federal Reserve Bulletin,* December 1993.

Table 2.5
**States Allowing Interstate Branch Banking before Passage of the Riegle-Neal
Interstate Banking and Branching Efficiency Act of 1994**

State Enacting Law	Effective Date of the Law	Area Covered and Reciprocity Requirement
Alaska	January 1, 1994	National, reciprocal
Massachusetts	Currently	National, reciprocal
Nevada	Currently	Permitted in those counties with less than 100,000 population
New York	Currently	National, reciprocal
North Carolina	Currently	National, reciprocal
Oregon	November 4, 1993	National, reciprocal
Rhode Island	Currently	National, reciprocal
Utah	Currently	National, no reciprocity

Source: Donald T. Savage, "Interstate Branching: A Status Report," *Federal Reserve Bulletin,*
December 1993; and Financial Structure Section of the Board of Governors of the Federal
Reserve System.

the Canadian banking system), competition could be damaged significantly.
The public might be faced with fewer options, higher fees, and poorer quality services. Moreover, the few remaining large banks might be tempted to
drain away local funds and place these monies in high-risk projects located
in distant markets that could lead to more bank failures. As will be shown
in the next chapter, the new interstate banking law of 1994 attempted to
address this danger by requiring interstate companies to pay attention to
the local credit needs of the cities and neighborhoods where their branches
are located.

However, even though the number of separately owned U.S. banks has
fallen by slightly more than a quarter over the past decade, small banks need
not be seriously threatened. Smaller institutions may be able to more closely
identify with particular local customer requirements better than larger banks
can do and pursue quality service more effectively, whereas larger banks
depend heavily upon greater service volume to maintain their profitability.
Then, too, bank customers may not be appreciably worse off in terms of
competitive options because, as seen in chapter 1, many more nonbank competitors have appeared recently to replace former banking competitors.
Among the most important of these nonbank competitors are savings and
loan associations, savings banks, and credit unions, who recently have been
granted many banklike services by government deregulation, while security
brokers and dealers, mutual funds, finance companies, and insurers offer
services that parallel many traditional banking services today, including consumer and commercial loans, savings plans, and cash management services.

At the same time both the Riegle-Neal Interstate Banking Act of 1994 and the Community Reinvestment Act of 1977 weigh against banks draining credit from local communities to concentrate their loans only in selected industries or regions. Allowing interstate full-service banking may actually increase competition. Therefore, service availability may become greater along with improvements in the efficiency of the American banking system. However, these potential benefits from the spread of full-service interstate banking are *not guaranteed*. They may sound plausible to be sure, but, at this point at least, the public service aspects of interstate banking remain essentially unconfirmed. The hope is that well-designed and sharply focused research will soon clarify what can be reasonably expected and not expected from the rise and growing dominance of interstate banking firms in the United States. A "taste" of what current research has to reveal about the behavior and performance of interstate banks will be offered in chapter 5.

CHAPTER 3

The 1994 Interstate Banking Law and Its Implications for the Structure of U.S. Banking

After more than half a century of outright prohibitions against interstate banking, a sweeping interstate holding company and interstate branching law finally passed the United States' Congress in the late summer of 1994. One key factor in the new law's passage was the banking and savings and loan crisis of the 1980s. This financial debacle resulted in the failure of more than two thousand depository institutions, bankrupted federal deposit insurance reserves, and reminded the public of the risks associated with financial-service firms that are narrowly dependent upon one community or even one state.

Moreover, as the 1980s began, federal banking agencies were given greater latitude to arrange cross-state mergers among failing and healthy banks and thrifts. This federally supported form of interstate banking helped to demonstrate to Congress and the public that interstate banking could bring public benefits in the form of recapitalizing and strengthening troubled banks and restoring public confidence in the nation's banking system. At the same time competition among nonbank financial-service firms had intensified, and several nationally focused nonbank financial institutions, particularly security dealers and mutual funds, were pulling away deposits from banks and savings and loan associations, making bankers aware that their markets had broadened substantially to include regional and even international components.

In this expanding and troubled financial marketplace artificial, legally imposed barriers to bank geographic expansion seemed less and less defensible. Then, too, the prospect that interstate banking firms could bring badly needed capital into economically troubled states and would pay attractive prices for the stock of targeted financial institutions helped to melt opposition from local bankers and legislators.

Another factor that surfaces from studying the dynamics of state branching laws during the 1930s has been the increasing mobility of bank customers. With millions of men and women crossing state lines to work and to shop each day, the artificial barrier represented by a state's territorial boundaries has seemed less and less relevant to daily business transactions. Moreover, the higher failure rates observed among smaller banks during the banking and savings and loan crisis of the 1980s caused Congress to reassess its attitude toward the emergence of large interstate banking firms, which seemed to offer greater stability and permanence to their customers along with a wider menu of financial-service choices.

THE RIEGLE-NEAL INTERSTATE BANKING AND BRANCHING EFFICIENCY ACT OF 1994

In 1991 the Treasury Department under the administration of President George Bush published a large scale research study of the potential benefits and costs of reforming the banking system and deregulating interstate banking. This study was entitled *Modernizing the Financial System: Recommendations for Safer, More Competitive Banks* (1991). As a result of heavy lobbying by bankers groups and extensive testimony from the managements of such leading banks as NationsBank, BankAmerica, Fleet, and Norwest, the Senate Banking Committee voted to deliver to the Senate floor an interstate banking bill on February 23, 1994, followed by the House Banking Committee on March 22, 1994. House and Senate conferees worked to iron out differences between the two chambers, which were subsequently approved by the full House on August 4 and by the entire Senate on September 13, 1994. The relatively speedy adoption of the Riegle-Neal law by both houses of Congress, after decades of no movement at all at the federal level, could be explained in part by the withdrawal of opposition by some powerful members of Congress to the idea of granting bankers interstate expansion powers without placing new and tougher limits on U.S. banks' other service powers (particularly on offering insurance services). With no apparent threats to banks' insurance powers, the banking industry was able to coalesce around support of the new bill, instead of remaining divided. The fear that deregulation of geographic expansion could be achieved only at significant political cost to the banking industry evaporated for a time, opening the door to the newest federal interstate banking and branching law.

Thus, by September 1994 what many industry observers said would not happen for at least another generation did happen: a federal interstate banking and branching bill passed by an overwhelming vote in both the U.S. House and Senate. On September 29, 1994, President Bill Clinton signed into law the Riegle-Neal Interstate Banking and Branching Efficiency Act during the final days of the 103rd Congress. (For a summary of this new law, see table 3.1.) In one stroke Congress had wiped away the restrictions against interstate expansion by bank holding companies as spelled out in the 1957 Douglas Amendment to the Bank Holding Company Act and the restrictions against branching across state lines originally laid down in the McFadden-Pepper (1927) and Glass-Steagall Acts (1933), discussed in chapter 2.

Table 3.1
The Riegle-Neal Interstate Banking and Branching Efficiency Act of 1994

INTERSTATE BANKING PROVISIONS

• Bank holding companies that are adequately capitalized and managed can acquire a bank anywhere in the United States one year after this law is enacted. However, no banking firm can acquire another banking firm in a different state if the resulting institution controls at least 30 percent of the insured deposits held in the state involved (though a state may waive or alter this limitation if it wishes) or as much as 10 percent of nationwide insured deposits. The states can protect *new* banks from acquisition by out-of-state firms for up to five years.

• Interstate bank holding companies that are adequately capitalized and managed may consolidate their affiliated banks acquired across state lines into branch offices via merger as early as June 1, 1997, unless the states act to outlaw interstate branching activity. An individual state may enact laws permitting interstate branching prior to June 1, 1997, and a host state that contains a branch office of an out-of-state bank can examine and take enforcement action against that branch office.

• If a state elects to prohibit interstate branching, banks headquartered in that state may *not* engage in interstate mergers.

• For those states involved in the interstate banking system, their regulatory agencies will be permitted to set up cooperative agreements to supervise multistate depository institutions.

• A federally insured bank can branch *de novo* into a state where it has no existing office but only if state law expressly permits *de novo* entry via branching. States can tax branches of out-of-state banks as if they were full-service banks operating in that state.

• Branch offices established across state lines to take deposits from the public must also create an adequate volume of loans (equal to half or more of the statewide average loan/deposit ratio) to support the local community or they may be closed. Interstate mergers and acquisitions are subject to mandatory review under the terms of the Community Reinvestment Act (CRA) to determine if the banks involved have a record of adequately serving their local communities. Written evaluations of an interstate bank's overall CRA performance and its performance in each state where it branches must be prepared by the appropriate federal agencies. Regulations prohibiting a bank from engaging in interstate branching primarily for the purpose of deposit production must be prepared and uniformly enforced by the federal banking agencies.

• Foreign-based banks may branch inside the United States on the same basis as domestic banks and are subject to review for their compliance with the CRA if they merge with domestic banks subject to the CRA. Foreign banks without U.S. deposit-taking offices must select a home state or, failing to do so, the Federal Reserve Board will designate their home state for purposes of regulation. National banks are subject to state law in the areas of community support, consumer protection, fair lending, and intrastate branching.

• Federal banking agencies must consult with community organizations before closing a branch office owned by an interstate banking company if the branch is located in a low- or moderate-income area.

Note:
The Riegle-Neal Interstate Banking and Branching Efficiency Act, signed September 29, 1994 as P. L. 703–3281, which repeals or amends sections of the Douglas Amendment and the McFadden Act.

Source: Pub. L. No. 103–328, 108 Stat. 2338; H.R. Conf. Rep. No. 651, 103d long., 2d. Sess. (1994).

The Riegle-Neal bill, named for its principal House and Senate sponsors, accomplished two major tasks:

1. It opened up the possibility of nationwide bank holding company acquisitions, beginning in September 1995, striking down any state laws that permitted the entry of banking companies only if they were headquartered in certain states or regions of the nation. The only significant limits that the Riegle-Neal bill introduced were a requirement that acquiring banking companies be adequately capitalized, as well as a national and state market-share constraint. Specifically, no interstate company could control more than 10 percent of nationwide insured deposits nor more than 30 percent of the total insured deposits in a single state (though the latter market-share constraint could be waived by state law or a state could choose another market-share limit). The 30 percent state limit does not apply to the first acquisition made in a given state nor to mergers involving already affiliated banking companies.

2. It allowed the conversion of banks acquired across state lines

into branch offices of interstate banking companies beginning June 1, 1997, though individual states could "opt out" of this new freedom of entry if they felt their domestic banking industry might be damaged. However, if a state does vote to "opt out" of interstate branching, its own banks cannot participate in interstate mergers. Individual states could vote to allow interstate branching earlier than June 1, 1997, if they wished to do so, however. Moreover, setting up new branches (as opposed to converting existing banks into branches) is permitted across state lines provided the states involved specifically authorize this form of market entry.

Recently two Washington, D.C., lawyers, Murray Indick and Satish M. Kini (1995), reviewed the options opened up to bankers under the 1994 Riegle-Neal Interstate Banking Act. They note that the new law actually imposes *two* tests on interstate companies seeking to expand across state lines:

1. An "adequately capitalized" test—which, by prior regulation emerging out of the Federal Deposit Insurance Corporation Act of 1991 (12 C. F. R. § 208.33), implies a ratio of total capital to total risk-weighted assets of at least 8 percent, a ratio of core (permanent) capital to risk-weighted assets of 4 percent, and a leverage ratio of no less than 4 percent.

2. An "adequately managed" test—which has not been previously defined either in law or regulation and must await the passage of time to become clearer as to what it means (or, more precisely, to determine what specific meaning, if any, the federal banking agencies will apply to this intriguing phrase).

Banks that appear to be failing or that have been declared to be insolvent represent exceptions to the above tests, as in earlier federal law under the Bank Merger and Bank Holding Company Acts and the Garn-St Germain Depository Institutions Act. Moreover, where failing banks are involved, interstate mergers or acquisitions sponsored by the FDIC cannot be blocked by the vote of a state authority.

Moreover, federal regulators are not entirely free to act as they wish even after the above tests are satisfied. States can protect their newest banks from interstate acquisitions up to a maximum of five years (as stated in Section 101[a] of Pub. L. No. 103–328). And federal authorities, before they act, must review to determine if a proposed interstate takeover would be in conformity with both federal and state antitrust and community reinvestment statutes.

The new law does help to clarify an issue that had hung over the industry for a long time—whether national (federally chartered) banks must play by the same interstate expansion rules as state-chartered banks when operating within the territory of a given state: Riegle-Neal generally answers that question in the affirmative, particularly where state rules for consumer protection and fair lending, community reinvestment, and intrastate branching are involved. In these instances Section 102(b) of Riegle-Neal says that state and federally chartered banks must conform to *state law* unless there is a preemptive federal law involved or national banks are being discriminated against (as determined by the Comptroller of the Currency). The branch of a national bank is to be treated the same way as if the national bank operating the branch were also based in the branch's home state.

Any state can vote before June 1, 1997, to prohibit mergers involving their banks with banks in other states, and the federal banking agencies cannot override such a vote. However, no state can discriminate against banks from any other state or group of states, allowing some outsiders to come in while excluding the entry of banks from other states. And a state prohibiting cross-border mergers and acquisitions cannot allow its own banks to reach across state lines in order to acquire banks in other states (unless a failing bank is involved). If a state had demanded prior commitments from out-of-state banking companies seeking to come into its territory (such as requiring the entering banking company to create new jobs or make a certain size commitment of new capital to the state), the Riegle-Neal law (in Section 102[a]) allows the states to require the bank holding companies making those commitments to honor them.

The United States Congress built in an automatic three-year delay—from August 1994, when Congressional passage occurred, to June 1997—before full-service interstate branching would be allowed. This delay had a specific purpose: to grant the states time to rewrite their tax laws so they could avoid losing substantial corporate tax revenues to the home states of out-of-state banking organizations. Currently, most superregional banking firms only pay taxes in their home states. Thus, many states will have to move away from the conventional franchise tax in order to be able to impose tax levies upon interstate banking organizations. By postponing the bank branching provisions until mid-1997, the states were granted at least two annual legislative sessions to address the corporate tax issues involved. (The state of Indiana apparently has already moved ahead of the other states with a 1990 law that taxes corporations on where they do business, rather than where they are incorporated.)

Under the Riegle-Neal bill "adequately capitalized" and "well-managed" bank holding companies could own a bank *anywhere* in the United States beginning one year after enactment of the law (starting on September 29,

1995), with Federal Reserve Board approval and regardless of any state laws to the contrary. After a bank is acquired by an interstate banking company, it may be converted into a branch office provided state law does not prohibit such a conversion and provided the conversion does not occur either prior to June 1, 1997, or before the time expressly permitted by state law. A banking company can acquire one or more branch offices of a bank in another state (without buying the whole bank) if the home state of the bank whose branches are being acquired approves of such an acquisition. In order to establish an interstate branching system by merger, however, the acquiring banking company, again, must be "adequately capitalized," and "adequately managed."

As noted earlier, once interstate holding-company affiliates are converted into branch offices, those branches must have an acceptable record of meeting the credit needs of the whole community they serve under federal and state community reinvestment laws. Otherwise, the interstate banking companies involved face the risk of having their branch offices closed by federal or state regulators. The federal regulatory agencies must consult with local community organizations, however, before they approve the closing of a branch office in a low-income area. Moreover, any proposed interstate branch offices may be prohibited from being established in those instances where an interstate company has a track record of poor performance in serving the local communities where it resides.

The new section of the Riegle-Neal bill applying to establishing bank branch offices across state lines is really an addendum to the Federal Deposit Insurance Act. This new addition to federal statutes (Section 44[a][1]) states:

> Beginning on June 1, 1997, the responsible agency may approve a merger transaction under Section 18(c) [of the Federal Deposit Insurance Act] between insured banks having different home states, without regard to whether such transaction is prohibited under the law of any state (Pub. L., No. 103–328, Section 102[a]).

Clearly this new branching provision of Riegle-Neal allows (a) mergers across state lines of previously unaffiliated banking firms; (b) the acquisition of a cross-border branch office offered by a selling bank (if the state involved approves); and (c) the consolidation of affiliated banks headquartered in different states into one consolidated banking entity, in which the affiliates are transformed into branch offices of a single company. However, *de novo* branching across state lines—that is, setting up new branch offices in a state where the bank involved has not been previously represented—can occur only if the state involved specifically decides to "opt in" to cross-border *de novo* branching (as stated in Pub. L. No. 103–328, Sec. 103). Otherwise, entry by acquisition of an existing banking entity is okay, but *de novo* branching activity is not.

While requiring express state approval for *de novo* branching is a clear disadvantage for interstate companies interested in entering new states with simple, lower-cost branch offices, one partially offsetting advantage is that the upper limits on deposit concentration of 10 percent nationwide and 30 percent at the state level are *not* applicable to expansion via *de novo* branch offices (though antitrust laws and community reinvestment laws still do come into play). However, once one *de novo* branch is approved, additional branches or mergers may occur statewide. And *no* interstate firm can set up a branch office merely to take deposits from a targeted local community without providing for that community's need for loans. For example, under federal regulation, the out-of-state banking firm's ratio of total loans to deposits in the state entered must be no less than half of the average loan-to-deposit ratio of home-state banks. If a federal regulator determines that a branch is not reasonably aiding a community to meet its credit needs, the regulator may order it closed in the state involved and new branches may not be permitted in any location (as stipulated in Section 109[c]).

The states may impose filing requirements on banking companies seeking to enter their territory. Both applicant banking firms and the federal banking agencies must honor these state filing requirements provided they are not discriminatory against out-of-state companies seeking to enter relative to what within-state banks or out-of-state nonbanking firms are allowed to do (as defined in Pub. L. No. 103–328, Sect. 102[a]).

However, state law cannot stop the Comptroller of the Currency from using the so-called leap-frog rule (Section 10[b] of the National Bank Act [12 U.S. C. § 10]) until June 1, 1997. This law allows a national bank to relocate its headquarters up to thirty miles away from its present site, even across state lines, with the approval of its stockholders and the Comptroller of the Currency. The old headquarters office is then simply converted into an ordinary branch office of the new headquarters.

Foreign banks can branch throughout the United States to the same extent as domestic banks, and foreign bank holding companies receiving approval from the Federal Reserve Board can acquire banks in any state. However, foreign banks that do not operate deposit-taking offices in the United States must choose a home state; otherwise the Federal Reserve Board will designate the foreign firm's home state for purposes of ascertaining the specific domestic laws and regulations that each foreign bank office in the United States must follow. If a foreign bank or bank holding company acquires or establishes a U.S. domestic bank that accepts deposits from the public, the foreign banking firm may become subject to the terms of the Community Reinvestment Act (CRA). Under this law, passed in 1977, both foreign and domestic banks must provide an adequate volume of loans and other services to their local communities without discrimination when they acquire a domestic banking firm that is subject to the requirements of CRA.

The Riegle-Neal bill allows affiliated banks to act as *agents* for interstate organizations in receiving and renewing deposits and in servicing and closing out loans. The "agency" power permitted by the Riegle-Neal interstate banking law was stated in the new law as an amendment to Section 18 of the Federal Deposit Insurance Act (12 U.S. C. at 1828). The new amendment simply stated:

> Any bank subsidiary of a bank holding company may receive deposits, renew time deposits, close loans, service loans, and receive payments on loans and other obligations as an agent for a depository institution affiliate. Notwithstanding any other provision of law, a bank acting as an agent in accordance with the provision above will *not* be considered to be a branch of the affiliate. [emphasis added]

This means that a separately incorporated bank affiliated with a bank holding company can function as a "de facto" branch office, allowing customers from other banking units of the same interstate organization to access their accounts through any bank affiliated with the same interstate company. These "agency services" can include receiving and renewing deposits, collecting loan payments, and closing out and servicing loans. Thus, the new law, potentially at least, increases the efficiency of multibank holding company organizations in order to allow them to more closely approach the service efficiency of branch banking organizations. While agency services have been provided by many banking companies in the past, the Riegle-Neal law places these services on a firm legal footing for the first time.

Agency powers, which became effective September 29, 1995, do not require specific regulatory approval. Moreover, the concentration limits and other state and federal rules that restrict interstate expansion via merger or acquisition generally do not apply to these new agency powers. However, it should be noted that when the Riegle-Neal bill was being debated, it was generally understood that these agency powers probably did *not* include setting up new accounts, evaluating and granting new loans, or dispensing borrowed funds. Thus, "agency" powers make affiliates belonging to the same banking company almost, but not quite, branch offices. Nevertheless, this new authority is important enough to forestall or slow some interstate banking companies from jumping right away into wholesale consolidation. Not all bank holding companies, at least for a time, will become fully integrated and consolidated financial-service firms even after all legislative and regulatory barriers are removed.

To be sure, some authorities believe that the new federal interstate banking law eventually will eliminate the future need for bank holding company–

type organizations. This is probably *not* true for a number of reasons. One is the continuing need to offer profitable services not currently allowed banks but that can be sold through the nonbank affiliates of a holding company. Another reason centers on the tough problem of how to enter a state that has refused to become a part of the interstate branching network. In this instance a bank holding company acquisition may be the only accessible legal option for entering a new state that has decided not to join the interstate branch office system. Finally, some bank customers may resent the loss of local autonomy if their banks are converted into mere branches of a distant bank headquartered in some other state or region of the country. These disgruntled customers may take their business to other banks that are locally owned—something that some interstate banks will almost certainly experience as interstate branch banking becomes a reality.

In summary, the 1994 Riegle-Neal interstate banking law allows banking firms to cross state lines through several different channels. Adequately capitalized and well-managed banks can acquire banks in states other than their home state beginning September 29, 1995. Holding-company-affiliated banks situated in different states can be combined into branch offices of a single interstate banking company—a process that can start no later than June 1, 1997. Alternatively, a banking organization can enter a state where it is not currently represented by setting up new branch offices if the state involved expressly gives its permission to create new branches (as opposed to converting existing acquired banks into branch facilities). Moreover, existing banks can operate in a given market as agents on behalf of holding-company-affiliated banks based elsewhere.

While the individual states were granted little influence over the first and last channels of bank expansion mentioned above, they were handed by the Congress considerable influence over interstate expansion via branching, as well as more time to react (until June 1, 1997) to possible bank branching activity that might take place across their borders. Each state can decide by a majority vote of its legislature or of its citizens whether it wishes to allow bank holding companies to convert their affiliated banks located within a given state's boundary lines into out-of-state controlled branch offices.

According to the American Bankers' Association (1995), seventeen states had taken a stand on interstate branching activity involving their own banks and territory in the first year following passage of the Riegle-Neal Interstate Banking Act. Texas voted earlier to opt out of the interstate system, at least in the initial years. Alabama, Connecticut, Delaware, Idaho, Illinois, Maryland, Nevada, New Hampshire, North Carolina, North Dakota, Oregon, Pennsylvania, Rhode Island, Tennessee, Utah, and Virginia have recently passed a variety of "opt in" laws applying to possible entry from the rest of the nation. A dozen of these states voted for entry by branching ahead of the Riegle-Neal law's trigger dates, while the remaining states (Illinois, New Hampshire, North Dakota, and Tennessee) set up new regulations that will govern interstate branching activity in their territory after the Riegle-Neal Act trigger dates take full effect. By April 1996, thirty-five states had opted into the interstate branching network including such recent additions as: Alaska, Arizona, California, Indiana, Maine, Michigan, Minnesota, Mississippi, New Jersey, New Mexico, New York, Oklahoma, South Dakota, Vermont, Washington, and West Virginia.

The Federal Reserve Board was also given key powers to limit and shape interstate bank expansion. The Federal Reserve can turn down any interstate holding-company acquisition that, in the Board's judgment, does not involve well-managed and adequately capitalized banks, violates antitrust or federal and state community reinvestment and consumer protection laws, or results in a level of deposit concentration that exceeds federal or state-imposed maximum percentages. However, if a troubled bank is involved, the board can approve an emergency interstate acquisition even if the acquisition fails to fulfill all of the regulatory-mandated guidelines.

Finally, as noted earlier, the Riegle-Neal interstate law allows an interstate banking company to set up *new* branches in any state that passes a law granting banking firms from other states permission to come in and set up new full-service facilities. The Riegle-Neal's definition of a *de novo* branch is any branch office that does not arise as the outcome of the acquisition of a bank or from a consolidation, conversion, or merger with another bank or branch office (as defined in 140 Congressional Record H6625–03, August 2, 1994). This final and ultimate step will be the most difficult one to achieve because many states are likely to be hesitant to make outside entry so easy (i.e., lower the costs of new market entry to such a low level). The power to set up brand new branch offices in the most promising new local market areas represents the greatest challenge to existing banks within a given state. While Riegle-Neal recognizes the preeminence of federal law in shaping the nation's banking structure (especially where national banks are involved), the new law requires federal authorities to seek public comment before issuing rulings that preempt state laws (particularly when the state laws involve consumer protection, fair lending, community reinvestment, or interstate branch banking).[1]

Moreover, the branch banking laws (as well as laws applying to consumer protection, fair lending, and community reinvestment) of a state entered by an interstate banking company apply to even the interstate branches of federally chartered (national) banks in the same way that they apply to the within-state branches of a state-chartered bank operating within its home state. Still, *de novo* branches of national banks appear to be exempt from state-conducted bank examinations. Moreover, any relevant state laws applying to the branch offices of an interstate national banking firm normally are to be enforced by the Administrator of National Banks (i.e., the Comptroller of the Currency). However, state laws apply fully and completely to the branching and other activities of interstate banks that are chartered by the individual states. For example, a state-chartered bank branching into a neighboring state must conform to all laws of the state entered, even if these laws are more restrictive than the laws of the bank's home state.

REGULATORY RELIEF AND THE COMMUNITY DEVELOPMENT AND REGULATORY IMPROVEMENT ACT OF 1994

Even as the U.S. Congress moved to open up interstate branching and nationwide holding-company banking it also acted in 1994 to ease the burden of federal regulations on industry reporting requirements. This was accomplished through passage of the Community Development and Regulatory Improvement Act of 1994, signed into law by President Clinton on September 23, 1994. (See table 3.2 for a summary of the major provisions of this law.)

Table 3.2
The Community Development and Regulatory Improvement Act of 1994

REDUCED REGULATORY BURDENS*

- U.S. banks will have to report fewer large currency transactions and may do so electronically to the U.S. Treasury Department under the amended Bank Secrecy Act. Financial institutions can submit lists of customers they wish to exempt from reporting requirements, but more large foreign transactions (including checks and money orders) must be reported. In cases of fraud or intentional misconduct, the FDIC and Resolution Trust Corporation can initiate claims against the management of failed institutions up to five years after a receiver or conservator is appointed.

- A bank's liability for deposits in a foreign branch where war, insurrection, civil strife, or sovereign action has occurred is limited.

- Federal bank regulatory agencies must eliminate outmoded or duplicative regulations that pose unwarranted restrictions on the growth of credit within two years of enactment of the law, and set up an appeals system so bankers can appeal regulatory decisions they feel are unfair. Agencies must appoint an ombudsmen between the banking agencies and those affected by banking agencies' regulations and seek out alternative methods for resolving disputes. The processing of bank applications is to be speeded up and streamlined (unless change of ownership is involved) and requests from more than one agency for duplicative information are to be eliminated.

- The thirty-day postapproval waiting period for mergers and acquisitions among depository institutions is reduced and the federal banking agencies need file a competitive factors report only if the proposed merger or acquisition raises competitiveness issues. Overall, the federal banking agencies must take final action on completed applications within a year of receipt.

- Federal banking agencies are to coordinate their examinations of depository institutions and develop a system for choosing a lead agency to carry out unified examinations.
- Only half the directors of a national bank must live within the headquarters' state or within one-hundred miles of the head office of the bank.
- Call reports of financial condition are to be simplified into a single form and can be filed electronically. The FDIC is directed to minimize the burden on well capitalized depository institutions of collecting and reporting deposit data.
- Small, well-managed, and well-capitalized banks not changing ownership (having total assets of less than $250 million and top-quality examiner ratings (that is, CAMEL 1 and 2 bank condition ratings) need be examined only once every eighteen months rather than once a year.
- Certain audit and reporting requirements can be satisfied at the holding company level for top-rated (CAMEL 1 and 2) banks.
- The federal banking agencies are allowed to establish guidelines for safety and soundness standards relating to operational and managerial areas, asset quality, earnings, and stock valuation instead of writing and enforcing these standards as required regulations.
- A Community Development Financial Institutions Fund is established in Washington, D.C., with $382 million in funds to provide financial and technical support to financial institutions and others promoting jobs and economic development in low- and moderate-income areas and among disadvantaged groups. Qualifying institutions can receive up to $5 million in any three-year period but must get matching funds from other sources unless this requirement is officially waived.
- A resale market for small business loans will be developed to encourage more lenders to support the creation and expansion of small firms. Banks and other lenders can secure small business loans and leases and commercial mortgages and invest in these securities.

Note:
* The Community Development and Regulatory Improvement Act, P. L. 103–325; signed September 23, 1994.

Prior to 1994, Congress had passed two highly restrictive bills in the form of the Financial Institutions Reform, Recovery, and Enforcement Act of 1989 (known as FIRREA) and the Federal Deposit Insurance Corporation Improvement Act of 1991 (known as FDICIA). These laws not only failed to grant new service powers and new territorial expansion powers to banks but imposed stiffer penalties for violations of federal banking laws, levied higher deposit insurance fees and increased capital requirements on banks and thrift institutions, and called for closer scrutiny of bank management policies and management quality. In fact, the FDIC Improvement Act required the FDIC to develop *management standards* for federally insured depository institutions in such areas as asset growth and quality, the payment of dividends, and the control of risk exposure. The management standards would also be used to check whether acceptable standards and policies were being followed when each bank and thrift institution was being scrutinized by federal examiners. In effect, the deregulation of U.S. banking that had begun with much fanfare in the early 1980s was stopped, and a return to a set of more restrictive rules ("reregulation") was ushered in by FIRREA and FDICIA. (See table 3.3 for a summary of major U.S. deregulation and re-regulation laws.) These new laws gave many bankers the impression that the clock of banking regulation had been turned back to the 1930s when Congress and the public feared a total collapse of the nation's banking system. Thus, the passage of the Riegle-Neal Bill and its companion law, the Community Development and Regulatory Improvement Act, was hailed by many bankers as a belated but welcome return to the deregulation era of the early 1980s.

Table 3.3
Deregulation and Reregulation of Banking in the United States

---

KEY DEREGULATION LAWS

The Depository Institutions Deregulation and Monetary Control Act of 1980

The legal ceiling rates on deposits sold to the public were to be gradually phased out by a Depository Institutions Deregulation Committee. Nonbank (federally supervised) depository institutions were granted broader new service powers, including credit cards, consumer installment loans, and commercial real estate loans. For example, federally insured credit unions were granted authority to offer real estate loans, while federally chartered savings and loan associations could offer credit cards, non-mortgage-related consumer loans, and trust accounts as well as purchase corporate bonds and notes up to a maximum of one-fifth of their total assets. Mutual savings banks chartered by the federal government were authorized to accept business loan requests from firms based in their own state or within a radius of seventy-five miles of the federal savings banks' home office. Federally insured banks, savings and loans, and credit unions were permitted to offer interest-bearing checking accounts to individuals and families as well as nonprofit institutions, and savings banks could sell checkable deposits to their business clients.

In order to improve the effectiveness of monetary control, the Federal Reserve Board was allowed to impose legal reserve requirements on all federally supervised depository institutions offering checkable deposits or nonpersonal time deposits. Nonbank thrift institutions that qualify could borrow from the Federal Reserve banks. The Federal Reserve was also authorized to begin charging depository institutions fees for using its services.

Garn-St Germain Depository Institutions Act of 1982

The new loan and deposit service powers granted nonbank thrift institutions by the Depository Institutions Deregulation Act of 1980 were further broadened, especially for consumer and commercial loans. Moreover, both banks and nonbank thrifts were granted authority to offer money market deposit accounts, bearing flexible, market-determined interest yields, in order to compete with the share accounts offered by money market mutual funds.

The so-called Garn bill allowed federally chartered thrifts to sell business checking accounts or make business payments on behalf of businesses with whom they had established a long-term customer relationship and to sell interest-bearing deposits to governmental entities. Further, both secured and unsecured loans could be extended to business firms provided that these credits did not total more than 10 percent of a federally chartered thrifts' total assets, and commercial real property loans could amount to as much as 40 percent of the assets of a federally chartered savings association. Those same thrift institutions could purchase state and local government bonds, whether revenue or general obligation (though the former could amount to no more than 10 percent of capital). Additional lending powers were also granted in the consumer area, with federally chartered savings associations allowed to make loans secured by personal property (provided these totaled no more than 10 percent of all their assets) and to grant consumer credit up to a maximum of 30 percent of each association's total footings.

KEY REREGULATING LAWS

Financial Institutions Reform, Recovery, and Enforcement Act of 1989

Civil and criminal penalties could be applied to managers and directors of banks and nonbank thrift institutions that violated federal banking laws. This act also restricted the service powers of thrift institutions and required these institutions to devote the majority of their asset portfolios to mortgage-related instruments in order to be qualified thrift lenders (QTLs) and receive tax reductions, low-cost federal loans, and other unique benefits. Dissolved the Federal Savings and Loan Insurance Corporation (FSLIC) and created the Savings Association Insurance Fund (SAIF), managed by the FDIC, to insure thrift deposits. Bank insurance reserves were placed under the control of the Bank Insurance Fund (BIF), also managed by the FDIC.

A new federal agency, the Office of Thrift Supervision (OTS), was created as part of the U.S. Treasury and was granted significant new regulatory powers over U.S. thrift institutions. For example, the OTS could order thrifts to slow their growth if their capital appeared to be inadequate, prohibit the taking of large, interest-sensitive deposits from security brokers and dealers, and outlaw thrifts' investments in junk bonds. Thrifts that accepted too much risk in their assets or operations could have their insurance coverage suspended. Federally insured thrifts deemed to have failed and taken over by the FDIC as receiver could have their assets liquidated by the Resolution Trust Corporation.

Federal Deposit Insurance Corporation Improvement Act of 1991

Recapitalized the FDIC and mandated increased deposit insurance fees until federal deposit insurance reserves held a minimum of $1.25 per $100 in covered deposits. Riskier banks and thrifts (as reflected in their capital adequacy and examiner ratings) must be assessed higher deposit insurance fees. The FDIC must develop and distribute management standards and policy statements to guide the management and policies of private banks and thrifts in dealing with asset growth, loan portfolio quality, dividend policies, risk management, and other serious management problem areas.

To aid the FDIC in finding healthy buyers of troubled depository institutions, savings associations and commercial banks may merge with each other.

Federal banking and thrift agencies could seize and sell or close a bank or thrift whose capital to tangible assets ratio dropped below 2 percent. As the capital position of a depository institution falls below minimum standards, federal regulatory agencies may impose limits on its growth, on the payment of shareholder or depositor dividends or interest, and may demand new management as well as restrict the acceptance of broker/dealer ("hot money") deposits. State-chartered but federally insured banks and thrifts cannot offer services or post lending limits not permitted to federally chartered depository institutions unless federal authorities find that these activities are not unsafe. However, federally chartered savings associations can expand their consumer loans up to 35 percent of their total assets.

Interestingly enough, however, bankers and the federal banking agencies often differ significantly in their assessment of how burdensome and costly U.S. banking rules and regulations are. One example of how differently regulators and regulated businesses can view the burden imposed by government rules occurred in the spring of 1996. The American Bankers Association (ABA) (1996) surveyed eighty-eight banks as to the amount of time they spent filling out consolidated reports of condition and income required during each quarter of the year. The ABA found that the average bank took 179 hours to complete its required September 1995 call (condition) report. In contrast, the FDIC estimated a total required time of only twenty-eight hours for state-chartered banks to complete its quarterly call report. The Federal Reserve Board estimated that only forty-four hours would be needed by state-chartered member banks to fill out the federal government's condition report, and the Comptroller of the Currency estimated that national banks could do the job in a mere thirty-eight hours.

On average, the ABA estimated that the typical U.S. bank spent close to $56,000 annually to prepare government-mandated call reports and that the time required to complete just one quarterly condition report ranged from 47 hours to as many as 440 hours. Suffice it to say that U.S. bankers as a group have had the distinct impression that the late 1980s and early 1990s were years of increasingly heavy reporting burdens and highly restrictive government rules.

Among the liberalizing steps passed into law in 1994 was a provision permitting federal examinations of adequately capitalized, relatively small banks to take place less frequently (every eighteen months instead of once a year) for top-examiner-rated banks holding up to $250 million in total assets. To be considered a top-rated bank an institution must receive a CAMEL score of one or two. (The acronym "CAMEL" refers to the capital adequacy, asset quality, management quality, efficiency, and liquidity ratings of each bank as determined by examiners from each bank's principal supervisory agency.) The CAMEL score can range from one (a top rating) to five for a bank in serious difficulty and believed to be headed for failure.) The smallest banks under $100 million in assets could also qualify for less frequent examinations if they received "above average" examination ratings (that is, CAMEL ratings of one or two). At the time the law was passed, an estimated nine thousand U.S. banks qualified for these less-frequent examinations.

For many banks today, one of the most burdensome regulations is the reporting to the U.S. Treasury of large cash transactions carried out by their customers. It is a time-consuming and invasive process, but under the new law, cash transactions over $10,000 would only have to be reported if the transaction involved a customer not well known to the bank. In April 1996 the Treasury Department reported that, effective May 1 of that year, most transactions with other U.S. banks and many corporations would no longer be subject to reporting unless cross-border transactions were involved. However, the Treasury deferred a final set of reporting rules for ninety days (as reported in *The Wall Street Journal*, April 18, 1996, p. C19). This provision will lead to an estimated 20 percent reduction in many banks' reporting work load.

An appeals system was set up to allow banks that felt they were the victims of discrimination in examinations or individual regulatory rulings to appeal and seek redress. The federal regulatory agencies were asked to respond significantly faster (generally within one year or less) to requests for official decisions, especially where mergers or acquisitions were involved. These agencies were directed to review and eliminate any outmoded rules still on their books within two years of the enactment of the new law.

Taking a step backward from the tough management rules laid down in FIRREA three years earlier, the new Regulatory Relief Act asks the federal banking agencies to merely issue "guidelines," instead of rigid rules, on bank asset quality, earnings, and equity value standards. The long-standing requirement to publish bank call reports in a local newspaper was lifted, and depository institutions were allowed to file their reports to the regulatory agencies electronically. Bankers' service corporations (known as *bankers' banks*) were permitted to offer correspondent services to bank holding companies, thus improving, potentially at least, the supply of correspondent services to smaller banks. Business deposits were exempted from the costly and time-consuming disclosure rules laid down in the Truth in Savings Act passed in 1991 and secured lending limits were extended.

On the local economic development side, a new community development financing system was created to make grants in aid in order to encourage economic development in the underdeveloped portions of local neighborhoods. Banks and other institutions would be eligible for small grants to improve local conditions and promote job growth. Unfortunately, only $382 million was allocated for this purpose over a four-year period. When spread over the hundreds of depressed areas around the United States, the total amount of funds available for each problem area would be, at best, a token amount. Nevertheless, the new community development law set up a Community Development Financial Institutions Fund, headquartered in Washington, D.C., and headed by a presidential appointee, to expand the supply of credit to low-income communities.

The funds to be allocated by the Community Development Fund were designed to be "seed money" for community development financial institutions (CDFIs). At the time the law was passed, there were CDFIs already operating in forty-five states with aggregate resources of about $1 billion. These institutions are principally *nonprofit lenders* with lending pools ranging from $200,000 to $35 million. In the long run the principal benefit of this new proviso for most commercial banks will be to reduce somewhat the pressure that many bankers feel today to devote more of their loan portfolio to low-income areas inside their local communities.

The 1994 law also called for the creation of a resale market for small business loans in order to support the expansion of credit flowing to these modest-size firms. Banks would be encouraged to invest in securitized pools of small business loans and commercial mortgages. Unfortunately, the Congress did not allocate funds to speed the development of a new market for selling business loans or for placing these loans in pools to support the issuance of securities, thereby generating more funds for capitalizing small businesses. Congress simply expressed the "wish" that small business loan markets would emerge, somewhat comparable to the huge resale and securitization markets for home mortgages that have taken nearly fifty years to develop and have been massively supported with federal government subsidies for decades.

Clearly, overall congressional support for the idea of developing a small business loan resale market is tepid at best. Indeed, given the highly variable terms of most small business loans, the creation of loan pools with acceptable features that would appeal to security investors represents no small challenge. Moreover, because small business borrowers often require close monitoring by banks (as well as technical advice from bankers along the way) to ensure that the terms of those loans are being followed, it may well be that these added costs will largely eliminate or override the benefits of securitization for both lenders and small businesses. It is not clear that a substantial and efficient small business loan market can be achieved anytime soon.

One step that may aid small business financing in the future, however, is a new bill introduced in the U.S. House of Representatives by Representative Baker (Republican of Louisiana) on February 28, 1996. The so-called Entrepreneurial Investment Act, which has received technical assistance in drafting from the staff of the Federal Reserve Board, would allow small bank holding companies (under $1 billion in assets) to invest in up to 25 percent of the stock of nonbank firms, provided the investment is a passive one (that is, the banking firm does not become involved in the management or operations of the nonbank business). The subsidiary banks of the investing holding company must be well capitalized, and the shares acquired cannot be directly or indirectly owned by a depository institution. Such a proposal, if passed, could be of significant help in capitalizing smaller businesses.

WHAT DID NOT PASS IN THE CONGRESSIONAL DEBATES AND WHY

While Congress took a major step toward nationwide banking in 1994, it has not been able to move toward a completely free and open banking system without restraints. As shown earlier in this chapter, the states were handed a possible "out" from the proposed interstate branching system. They could block out-of-state companies from converting banks headquartered in their territory into branch offices. Congress also failed to amend the Glass-Steagall Act's prohibitions against the investment banking activities of commercial banks where corporate debt and stock is involved, leaving that step to the case-by-case review process begun by the Federal Reserve Board in the 1980s. While two earlier bills, H.R. 1062 and 1858, both calling for repeal of Glass-Steagall's restrictions against investment banking, were combined into one bill, H.R. 2520, the proposed Financial Services Modernization and Regulatory Burden Relief Act, no action has occurred since these bills were introduced in committee in January of 1995.

Moreover, while many U.S. banks have sought insurance powers, Congress also did *not* act to open up the insurance market, due in part to an intense lobbying effort from the life and property-casualty insurance industry. Progress toward greater bank involvement in the insurance industry seems to rest more upon the U.S. courts than upon the probable actions of legislative bodies. For example, on March 26, 1996, the U.S. Supreme Court in *Barnett Bank of Marion County, N.A. v. Nelson* (U.S. Sup. Ct. No. 94–1837) ruled that the states cannot prevent national banks from engaging in insurance sales in small towns (having populations of less than five thousand), allowing national banks to operate insurance agencies if they wish.

Thus, the pattern of prior U.S. banking history in which legislation and regulation only seem to change one step at a time seems to have largely continued in the 1994 federal interstate banking legislation. Confronted with strong conflicts from competing financial-service industries, Congress was able to take one step forward toward significant geographic deregulation, but further steps, especially in product-line deregulation, must await future legislative sessions or court decisions.

Both the U.S. House and Senate also rejected the Fair Trade in Financial Services Act proposed at about the same time. This proposed law would permit federal agencies to block the expansion of foreign-owned financial-service firms inside the United States if the home nations of those foreign firms are placing damaging restrictions on U.S. companies. This bill did not pass, in part because of concern about damaging the American bargaining position regarding trade liberalization around the globe.

More important for the interstate banking movement, the Riegle-Neal Interstate Banking Act did *not* resolve how the states will be impacted by a potential loss of tax revenue. When only bank holding companies were the principal type of interstate banking organization, the states could easily tax each affiliated bank situated within their borders because each bank affiliate is a separate corporation and must report its profits separately from the holding company that controls its stock. Now many, if not most, states will have to adjust their laws to be able to levy new taxes and fees against bank branch offices. This will not be easy because clever managers may find a way to move profits from heavily taxed units to those affiliated entities in another state that are more lightly taxed—a problem analogous to the transfer pricing schemes used today by some international corporations to avoid taxation by high-tax-rate nations.

Another partially unresolved issue centers around federal and state bank examination powers, as noted by banking professor Dr. Edward J. Kane (1995). The Riegle-Neal bill states that national banks will be examined by the Comptroller of the Currency's staff, regardless of which state is their home base and irrespective of any other states they may have entered. State-chartered banks, in contrast, are subject to examination by their home state. However, suppose a state-chartered bank in Massachusetts establishes branch offices in California. The California branches then become subject to California banking laws. California's banking authorities, presumably, could legally examine and supervise the Massachusetts' bank's branch offices. The argument here is that branch offices located in any particular state should receive "equal treatment" with the offices of any other banks that call that state home.

However, this neat little scheme raises a potentially nasty problem. Suppose supervisors from the states entered (in the example above, California) become concerned about a bank's overall stability and future viability, but its home-state examining agency (in the case above, the Massachusetts' banking commission) does not express any concern. How far can an individual state's examiners go? Can a state containing only a few branch offices of a large interstate organization launch an investigation of the *whole* interstate company? And, as Kane (1995) notes, if a state-chartered bank *is* properly subject to supervision by several states, would it not have a substantial incentive to convert to a national bank, which faces only one principal supervisor (the Comptroller of the Currency)? In truth, several states have expressed concern that many state-chartered banks will leave the state supervisory system and join the national banking system because of the latter's comparative uniformity. Under the state system a new and somewhat different set of rules confronts a state-chartered interstate bank every time it enters a new state. At least some state-based banking companies will find this an onerous burden and, presumably, opt for the federal banking system.

FUTURE REGULATORY REFORM

Until the 1990s the pace of regulatory reform in the banking and financial institutions field was slow and deliberate. Major banking bills were seen once or twice per decade. However, the rapidly advancing technology of information gathering and communication appears to have brought the public closer to the regulatory process and more sensitive to its successes and short-comings. The hoped-for outcome will be more rapid adjustments of regulatory regimes and processes in the future in an effort to keep pace with the shifting demands of the financial-services marketplace and with improvements in the technology of producing and delivering financial services.

However, there are no certainties when it comes to legislative and regulatory reform, especially in the face of continuing competitive conflicts between commercial banks and nonbank financial-service providers, such as insurance companies and security dealers. The active opposition of these and other parties of interest may continue to frustrate further banking industry reforms despite ongoing changes in the public's financial-service needs and in the technologies surrounding the delivery of banking services.

To the extent that banking firms cannot effectively blunt the damage caused by slowly adjusting laws and regulations, their industry is in serious danger of becoming increasingly irrelevant to the public's financial-service demands. Already, in the face of the Glass-Steagall Act's prohibitions against the general offering of underwriting services for privately issued securities, commercial banking's share of U.S. credit markets appears to have declined somewhat over the past two decades. The same fate may befall other key bank service lines in the absence of regulatory relief until the commercial banking industry as it is known today ceases to play a substantive role in the workings of the financial system.

NOTE

1. The Riegle-Neal Interstate Banking Act has not been the only example of federal laws that can preempt the states' authority over banks entering their territory in favor of federal authority. As Darrel Dreher, Hugh Hayden, and Michael Tomkies (1995) note, the late 1980s and early 1990s ushered in a wide array of court decisions and regulatory pronouncements that allow lenders situated in one state to extend credit to borrowers located in other states on terms (particularly interest rates and fees) that are allowed by the lenders' states but not necessarily by the borrowers' states. In other words, lenders can "export" the terms of a loan at their permissible rates and fees even if the borrowers' states outlaw these lenders' rates and fees. In

this instance, federal rules allow the preemption of state law. Moreover, the courts have generally held that fees are part of the interest on a loan. Among the significant cases in this area are *Greenwood Trust Co. v. Massachusetts* (776 F. Supp. 21 [D. Mass 1991] and 971 F. 2d at 818), *Ament v. PNC National Bank* (849 F. Supp. 1015), and *Smiley v. Citibank South Dakota, N.A.* (32 California Reptr. 2d 562). In the foregoing cases the courts have generally held that a loan originates with the lender's decision to extend credit and that decision is made on the lender's premises. Thus, the law that prevails at the lender's site, not the borrower's site, determines whether loan terms are within the permitted range.

CHAPTER 4

The Potential Benefits and Costs of Interstate Banking

Will interstate banking and branching bring substantial benefits to the public and to American banking as a whole, or result in substantial costs and risks to bank customers and a burden to an industry caught in the midst of change? No one knows for sure, but several ideas have emerged about what the future may bring to American banking and to the businesses and individuals it strives to serve. This chapter looks at the expected benefits and costs that may lie ahead as the industry experiences one of the most basic structural changes in its history.

THE ACTUAL AND POTENTIAL BENEFITS OF INTERSTATE EXPANSION

In a 1993 study conducted by the General Accounting Office (GAO)— a prelude to the consideration of new interstate banking legislation by the U.S. Congress—the GAO (1993) concluded that interstate banking activities have contributed to a substantial consolidation of the U.S. banking industry and have resulted in an increase in overall industry concentration. However, the GAO could find *no* direct relationship between increased interstate banking activity and changes in banking concentration at state and local levels (measured by the proportion of local banking assets held by the three largest banking firms). To the contrary, the GAO argued that the roles played by smaller banks (defined as those under $1 billion in assets) would be little affected by the spread of interstate activity. In its opinion, smaller banks would maintain their industry share (about 10 percent of all U.S. banking assets), and some might even gain a greater share (as happened in nine of sixteen states examined by the GAO where there was a substantial interstate banking presence).

The Government Accounting Office concluded that eventual passage of new federal interstate banking legislation would increase the nationwide concentration in U.S. banking, but would not necessarily increase concentration or damage competition in local cities and counties around the nation. Moreover, removing legal barriers to crossing state lines might enhance the industry's safety and soundness and benefit certain customer groups. If interstate banking does bring added risks to bank solvency, however, the GAO argued that this problem could be dealt with by restricting approvals of interstate bank expansion to well-managed and well-capitalized banks and through vigorous enforcement of antitrust, fair lending, and affirmative action laws (such as the Community Reinvestment Act). In brief, whatever risks may lie ahead because of interstate expansion, the GAO argued that sufficient federal and state laws were already in place to deal adequately with these risks.

In effect, the Government Accounting Office is suggesting that interstate banking is likely to be a mixed blessing for the United States, offering both potential benefits and possible costs. Among the most frequently cited potential benefits are greater service convenience for the public, the availability of a wider menu of services, increased service innovation, improved bank operating efficiency, greater bank safety and stability, and improved regulatory efficiency in managing a more consolidated banking system. The most widely predicted costs include the possibility of greater consolidation of the nation's banking resources (and, therefore, diminished competition), higher prices and fees charged the public for financial services, less credit availability for small businesses, excessive returns for some bank stockholders, possible loss of state and local tax revenues and control by the individual states over their own banking systems, job losses in the banking sector, branch closings and reduced customer convenience, threats to the survival of small banks, and the potential loss of local influence over bank policies and decisions. This chapter examines each of these contentions briefly. Chapter 5 will explore the research evidence for and against many of these claims.

Greater Service Convenience for Traveling Customers

One of the strongest arguments made for interstate banking in recent years has centered around the mobility of Americans. It has been estimated that about sixty million Americans—approximately one-quarter of the nation's population—cross the borders of one state and enter another en route to their place of work, to school, or to shopping each day. Many of these individuals live in one state but bank in a neighboring state. To these bank customers, the *portability* of financial services—particularly access to one's checking and credit or savings account across state lines—is highly important. Add to these mobile customers the millions of other Americans who travel on business trips from one part of the United States to another as well as overseas each day and you have a substantial segment of the U.S. population interested in convenient access to financial services no matter where business or pleasure takes them.

Presumably, as more banks establish or acquire control of offices across state lines, it will become easier for a traveling customer to access his or her funds through different facilities of the same bank rather than from banks under different ownership and control. Customer transactions should be simpler to carry out and less costly for both customers and their depository institutions. In a sense, *increased customer mobility has created the demand and the political agenda for the expansion of interstate banking in the United States.*

Wider Service Menus Available through Existing Production Units

One of the most frequently claimed benefits associated with interstate banking lies in the, presumably, greater availability of banking services, particularly to smaller local communities who may be "underbanked" and underserved. Generally, when a bank expands in size, its service menu grows as well. This tendency of banks to engage in "service proliferation" over time seems to occur for several reasons:

1. increases in bank resources that come with size and growth allow bank managers to do more things, including the diversion of more resources into new service development;

2. larger banks can withstand the greater risks inherent in offering new services; and

3. as a bank expands in size, it usually enters new market areas whose service needs may differ somewhat from the service needs of market areas previously served, leading to a widening service menu in both old and new market areas.

By opening up new local markets, banks that go interstate allegedly can outgrow most intrastate banks, resulting in an expansion of service availability to the public. Moreover, when an interstate bank expands its service menu, it can offer those same services through most, if not all, of its existing offices and facilities. The result *may* be a net gain in service convenience (i.e., lower transactions cost) for the public, which, over time, should spread across the nation.

Several interstate banking firms have recently argued that service offerings *must* increase as a result of interstate mergers and acquisitions because of the service requirements inherent in the Community Reinvestment Act, passed in 1977. As described briefly in chapter 3, this widely publicized federal law requires banks operating deposit-taking facilities in local communities to pledge to offer their services throughout their designated trade territories without discriminating against certain neighborhoods (known as "redlining"). Federal bank regulatory agencies have become especially watchful of the treatment of customers seeking home mortgage credit to insure there is no pattern of denials of loan applications based upon the geographic location of the borrower's proposed home or place of business. Indeed, the Home Mortgage Disclosure Act passed in 1978 requires covered lending institutions (which includes all federally supervised banks) to report the location, race, and other pertinent data of borrowers seeking home loans in order to make it easier for regulators to spot credit discrimination.

Both the federal bank regulatory agencies and several state banking commissions have been largely successful at wringing pledges from merging banks to increase their credit support for small businesses and home loan customers, for nonprofit community organizations, and for areas in need of expanding job opportunities. For example, when Chemical Banking Corporation and Chase Manhattan proposed to merge in 1995, these two banks unveiled an $18 billion community loan package, covering a five-year period with pledges of financial support in the form of loans and investments for small businesses, nonprofit organizations, and new home buyers in their combined service area.

In the current era of rapid technological change, interstate banks may be better positioned, resource- and stability-wise, to identify and successfully pursue new product development. Today the most promising new service areas in banking encompass investment products (such as offerings to families concerned about retirement, rising college costs, and other long-run funding needs of mutual funds and annuities) and lower-cost service delivery channels (e.g., remote access to bank service facilities through personal computers, the telephone, the World Wide Web, electronic cash cards, and other emerging information storage and retrieval technologies). The argument here is that an interstate organization can increase its revenues by entering new markets with its existing menu of services and by developing new products (i.e., service diversification) that can be offered in both old and new market areas. If revenues from new services do not also bring a fully commensurate increase in operating costs, organizational profits will increase. Indeed, recent research by Benston, Hunter, and Wall (1995) suggests that this so-called revenue effect from recent bank mergers may help explain why acquiring banking companies often pay more to purchase small banks than they do to buy larger ones. The strategy of acquiring smaller banks may give interstate acquirers greater opportunities to offer *new* services that smaller banks previously could not offer to their customers due to the costs and risks of service innovation.

Improved Bank Efficiency, Leading to Lower Prices for the Public

Interstate banking, particularly if banks acquired across state borders can be consolidated into simple branch offices, *may* lead to more cost-efficient banks. Bankers have argued that the consolidation of hundreds of individual banks into nationwide branch networks would significantly lower the banking industry's *noninterest costs* (i.e., wages, salaries, and overhead expenses). These savings are most likely to come from such sources as consolidation of portfolio management and risk protection services, more efficient transactions processing, elimination of duplicate boards of directors and management among affiliated banks, and integration of public relations and marketing strategies. If competition is sufficiently intense, these cost savings *may* be passed on to the public in the form of lower service fees. However, it is important not to overstress these possible cost savings resulting from the expansion of interstate banking. Recent experience suggests they are likely to be far less than expected.

For example, as E. Laderman (1995) observes, studies comparing merging banks with nonmerging institutions generally do *not* find that mergers (including both interstate and noninterstate) have lowered bank operating costs, on average. This also seems to be true in some cases when two banking companies that have overlapping branch office networks merge and are, therefore, able to close some branch offices in order to eliminate duplication. Moreover, studies of bank cost curves (which relate unit operating costs to changes in total bank output or assets) generally find that the lowest cost point, where the average cost per unit of output is at a minimum, tends to occur at relatively low levels of bank output. That is, based on recent cost studies, the lowest-cost bank may be no more than moderate size (perhaps between $60 million and $500 million in total assets), which is far smaller than most of the leading interstate banks today. One contrary note, however: a recent study by Wheelock and Wilson (1994) of productivity changes in U.S. banking over the 1984–93 period finds that American banks with assets exceeding $300 million (in constant 1985 dollars) became *more* productive during the mid-1980s and early 1990s, while banks smaller than $300 million became *less* productive and *less* efficient, on average, as declines in technical efficiency offset the impact of the technical progress the smaller banks had made. Thus, on balance, larger U.S. banks over the period examined apparently adapted better to changes in technology than did smaller American banks, something chapter 5 will examine more deeply.

Improved Bank Safety and Stability

The failure rate among larger American banks, historically, is appreciably lower than among smaller banking firms, which are often heavily dependent upon a single, relatively small market area. Because this large-bank advantage has persisted for many decades, the public, especially large depositors not fully protected by federal deposit insurance, seem to be aware of this difference in stability and tend to direct the largest transactions and thrift accounts toward larger financial-service companies. There is often a detectable shift in the public's funds toward larger financial institutions in times of stress within the banking system, especially when the bank failure rate moves higher. Presumably, the growth of interstate banks would increase public confidence in the safety and stability of the banking system, though, as will be shown later in this chapter, that growth may also result in less insurance protection for the largest depositors.

Improved Regulatory Efficiency in Managing a More Consolidated Banking System

There may be a gain in the efficiency and effectiveness of banking regulation in an interstate-bank-dominated banking system. To the extent that interstate banking leads to a more consolidated banking system—fewer numbers of banks and much larger banking institutions on average—there are fewer individual banking firms to be examined and regulated. Scarce regulatory resources can more easily be focused on the most troubled banking firms, increasing the efficiency and, possibly, the effectiveness of government regulation of the banking industry. A potential offsetting cost, however, is the growing complexity of the largest interstate banking companies, which may make it harder for regulators to detect serious problems in time.

ACTUAL AND POTENTIAL COSTS OF INTERSTATE BANKING

If the foregoing are potential benefits of interstate banking, what then are its possible costs?

Growing Concentration of the Public's Deposits in the Largest Banking Firms at the National Level and within Individual States

One structural trend in U.S. banking that seems to be directly related to the rise of interstate banking is an increasing concentration of industry re-

Table 4.1
Proportion of U.S. Bank Assets Held by Out-of-State Banking Organizations

Year	Share of U.S. Banking Assets or Deposits in Banks Owned by Out-of-State Banking Organizations (in percent)	Share of U.S. Commercial Banking Assets Open to Out-of-State Ownership (in percent)
1987	10.59	91.69
1988	13.72	96.11
1989	15.32	96.98
1990	15.88	97.37
1991	16.89	98.51
1992	19.74	99.28
1993	24.56[1]	99.49
1994	24.43[1]	99.53
September 1995	27.10[1]	99.55[2]

Notes:
Includes only insured domestic commercial banking assets. Special purpose banks are excluded.
[1] Changed to domestic deposits rather than assets due to the existence of some interstate branching.
[2] Figures as of June 1995.

Sources: Data are from tables constructed for December of each year. Structure reflects acquisitions that have been approved by the Board and published in the *Federal Reserve Bulletin* by December. Asset data are based in September call reports. For September 1995, structure data reflects acquisitions published in the *Federal Reserve Bulletin* by September 1995, and financial data are for June 1995. September 1995 data include interstate branches as of September 1995 using summary of deposits data for June 1994. Presented in Janet L. Yellen, Testimony before the Subcommittee on Financial Institutions and Consumer Credit, U.S. House of Representatives, October 17, 1995.

sources in the largest banks. The share of domestic assets held by the largest one hundred U.S. banking companies reached nearly 72 percent in the summer of 1995, compared to about 51 percent in 1980. This rapid rise in industry share occurred over the period of most intense structural change in American banking—the 1980–95 period—when more than six thousand banks were absorbed by merger and just over fifteen hundred bank failures occurred.

Moreover, out-of-state banking organizations are controlling a growing share of the banking assets and deposits held inside each state. Overall, as table 4.1 shows, out-of-state banking organizations controlled just over 27 percent of the deposits of all U.S. banks in September of 1995—a figure that has nearly doubled since 1988. And, with recent changes in both state and federal laws, nearly all U.S. banking assets (99.55 percent) were available for possible purchase by out-of-state banking organizations by 1995. Clearly, there is plenty of added room for interstate banking organizations

Table 4.2

Proportion of Domestic Bank Deposits in Each State that Are Controlled by Interstate Banking Companies Based in Other States (as of June 30, 1993)

States	Percent of Domestic Bank Deposits in Insured Commercial Banks Controlled by Out-of-State Holding Companies	States	Percent of Domestic Bank Deposits in Insured Commercial Banks Controlled by Out-of-State Holding Companies	States	Percent of Domestic Bank Deposits in Insured Commercial Banks Controlled by Out-of-State Holding Companies
Alabama	3.2	Louisiana	5.3	Ohio	3.4
Alaska	23.6	Maine	78.2	Oklahoma	12.7
Arizona	89.7	Maryland	24.6	Oregon	48.2
Arkansas	2.0	Massachusetts	29.8	Pennsylvania	10.7
California	2.2	Michigan	3.6	Rhode Island	26.9
Colorado	56.9	Minnesota	3.2	South Carolina	64.2
Connecticut	49.4	Mississippi	2.2	South Dakota	53.0
Delaware	38.0	Missouri	0.2	Tennessee	29.5
Florida	50.0	Montana	31.1	Texas	53.0
Georgia	42.2	Nebraska	10.2	Utah	27.5
Hawaii	8.4	Nevada	89.4	Vermont	4.4
Idaho	56.7	New Hampshire	23.4	Virginia	39.7
Illinois	15.3	New Jersey	21.1	Washington	81.2
Indiana	53.4	New Mexico	32.9	West Virginia	27.0
Iowa	23.2	New York	6.5	Wisconsin	16.7
Kansas	10.2	North Carolina	0.3	Wyoming	53.6
Kentucky	35.4	North Dakota	30.7	Washington, D.C.	58.7

National Average Percent of Each States Deposits Controlled by Out-of-State Bank Holding Companies: 22.8%

Notes:

Figures exclude foreign-owned banks, special-purpose banks, nonbank banks, and nondeposit trust companies but do include foreign bank holding companies with banking subsidiaries in at least two states.

Sources: Federal Deposit Insurance Corporation, Reports of Condition, all insured banks; and Donald T. Savage, "Interstate Banking: A Status Report," *Federal Reserve Bulletin,* December 1993, p. 1084.

to grow as economic and regulatory pressures build to support territorial expansion.

At the individual state level there are several states where out-of-state banking firms control a majority of the domestic deposits. For example, as table 4.2 shows, out-of-state banking companies in Arizona, Nevada, and Washington controlled more than 80 percent of statewide domestic deposits in June 1993. Not far behind was Maine, where more than three-quarters of all domestic deposits were managed by out-of-state-owned banks. In thirteen states, banking companies owned by out-of-state investors accounted for half or more of all domestic deposits in the summer of 1993, indicating growing concentration of the public's deposits at least within these particular

Table 4.3
Arguments Typically Advanced for and against Interstate Banking

Alleged Advantages/Benefits Associated with Interstate Banking	*Alleged Disadvantages/Costs Associated with Interstate Banking*
Greater service convenience for traveling customers	Growing concentration of the public's deposits in the largest banks at the national level and within individual states
Wider service menus available to the public	Higher service fees as service pricing schedules are altered to reflect the policies of the acquiring firm
Increased innovation in service production and delivery	Fewer loans and higher service prices for small businesses as competitors merge across state and regions
Improved bank efficiency, leading to lower prices for the public	Abnormal excess returns for acquired bank shareholders as their stock is sold to interstate acquirers
Improved bank safety and stability and reduced failure risk	Possible loss of state tax revenues and control over each state's banking structure
Improved regulatory efficiency in managing a more consolidated banking system where there are fewer banks for regulators to monitor	Bank employee layoffs
	Branch office closings and reduced customer convenience
	Survival pressures on small banks and their stockholders
	Loss of local influence and local control over bank policies and credit decisions
	Loss of some federal insurance coverage on some deposits as formerly independent banks are merged into one bank

states—one of the possible disadvantages of spreading interstate banking as summarized in table 4.3.

Of course, the presence of fewer banking companies facing the consumer of banking services does not necessarily mean that consolidation of banking units will diminish competition. The U.S. banking industry represents only about 35 percent of the total assets of all financial-service firms serving U.S. markets today. Competition from a wide array of other financial-service suppliers, led by securities and insurance firms (such as Merrill Lynch, Prudential, Fidelity Investments, and Dreyfus Corporation) has been increasing rapidly and, by some measures at least, banks have lost market share to these highly competitive businesses. Thus, trends in bank numbers and bank deposit concentration do *not* tell the whole story of how the public will be impacted by the current consolidation trend sweeping through American banking and, particularly, by the continuing expansion of interstate banking.

Higher Fees Charged the Public for Banking Services

There is a widespread belief that the takeover of one bank by another generally results in the public being assessed *higher* service charges for access to banking services, especially for access to checking account services, for conducting transactions through an ATM or other automated facility, and for access to credit. Thus, it is widely believed that most bank mergers result in little or no benefit for consumers. Such a belief is, at least, consistent with the notion that bank mergers and acquisitions diminish competition.

However, an equally plausible explanation for why service fees often rise after banks are acquired is that larger bank acquirers often have more sophisticated cost accounting systems that reveal the full cost of offering their services and, therefore, are more likely to actively seek to recover that cost. Bank executives often argue that service fees don't automatically rise in the wake of a merger but that market conditions, particularly the intensity of competition, are the primary determinants of which direction bank service fees will move. Of course, in those mergers where former competitors serving the same market areas agree to combine, this eliminates one competitor and one alternative, independent source of supply of financial services. If consolidation of this sort leads to a significant decline in competition, bank service fees may, indeed, rise once a merger is consummated, whether that merger is intrastate in nature or crosses state boundaries.

Fewer Loans and Higher Service Prices for Small Businesses

One of the greatest concerns in Congress and among consumer groups regarding the spread of interstate banking is its possible impact on the *small business* sector. There is a popular belief that, as banking organizations grow larger, they tend to make fewer loans available to selected groups or, at least, the proportion of their loans flowing to certain sectors of the economy tends to decrease. Prominent examples include agricultural loans and loans extended to new or newly emerging businesses. The fear in this case is that an expansion of interstate banking might well lead to more credit for large corporations and less for the smaller firms that account for much of the new job growth in the U.S. economy each year.

This is an especially critical allegation because, outside of commercial banks, small businesses often find few other places to go to raise working capital or to fund the long-term expansion of their business. Some near-bank institutions—for example, savings and loan associations and credit unions—make business loans (as observed, for example, by Hannan and Liang [1995]) as a result of federal deregulation legislation during the 1980s, but their overall market share is still small.

Moreover, there appears to be only limited potential for developing a securitization market for small business loans, even though the U.S. Congress called for the development of such a market in 1994 (as noted in chapter 3). Recently, Benston (1992) and Beshouri and Nigro (1994) have concluded that the special characteristics of small business finance impose costs that may swamp the usual benefits of securitization and inhibit the development of a small secondary market for many years to come. Thus, in the absence of new government programs or greater involvement by specialized business lenders, smaller businesses are likely to remain heavily dependent upon commercial banks as their primary source of working capital and equipment loans for the foreseeable future. If interstate banks do tend to divert credit from small to large companies, smaller businesses will have to find more of their capital from sources other than the banking sector, which may result in both less credit availability and more expensive credit for this important sector of the U.S. economy.

Abnormal Excess Returns for Acquired Bank Shareholders

It is frequently contended that interstate acquisitions have resulted in *excess returns* for the stockholders of banks and bank holding companies targeted for acquisition. Allegedly, the shareholders of banks and bank holding companies that are acquisition targets will enjoy a double benefit: (a) rates of return in excess of what would normally be expected on other investments of comparable risk (at least for a short period of time around the date of the acquisition) and (b) increased liquidity of the stock they ultimately hold because the stock of a smaller bank or bank holding company (the acquired firm) is usually exchanged for the stock of the larger banking firm (the acquirer). The excess returns arise, in part, because acquired banks have a charter value due to government restrictions on entry into the banking industry that leads capital market investors to believe that protected banks will be able to generate abnormal profits in the future.

A more difficult question yet to be resolved is: What are the financial benefits to the *acquirer* and its shareholders? As the next chapter will show, the research evidence is decidedly mixed with regard to any gains experienced by interstate acquirers, who often appear to pay too much for their acquisition targets and require several years to recoup acquisition costs from their profits. Nevertheless, there is little dispute today over the fact that the principal beneficiaries in nearly all interstate acquisitions to date have been the stockholders of the banking firms *acquired* by interstate banks.

Possible Loss of State Tax Revenues and Control of Banks within State Borders

The spread of interstate banking *may* present the states with substantial losses in tax revenues. Currently the tax structures of most states levy taxes against the headquarters of the firms operating within their borders. As banking affiliates situated in states other than the home state of the controlling banking company are converted from separate corporations into branch offices, the states where those branches are situated may have little or no authority to tax the bank that controls them. A few states (for example, Indiana) have recently moved to remedy this situation, however, by altering their tax codes to allow taxation of the sales of branch offices housed within their territory. However, most states are not fully prepared for the impending expansion of interstate banking.

Moreover, expansion of interstate banking under federal rules may mean that the banking structure in any particular state is more likely to mirror the industry's structure nationally rather than reflecting the character of different regions of the country. Thus, individual state governments will experience less and less control over the makeup of the banking industry within their borders with the passage of time. Increasingly, bankers interested in geographic expansion will seek their cues from the federal banking agencies— the FDIC, the Federal Reserve, and the Comptroller of the Currency— rather than state bank regulatory agencies and state influence on the organization of the nation's banking industry has declined and will likely decline further in the future.

Bank Employee Layoffs

As the number of banks continues to fall, many bankers foresee a continuing shrinkage in the number of bank employees, especially with continuing advances in information and service delivery technology, which tend to expand the role of capital equipment, making those employees who do remain more productive. Indeed, bank megamergers in the 1980s and early 1990s led to large-scale layoffs at several leading money-center banks. For example, when Chemical New York Corp. acquired Manufacturers Hanover in New York, close to six thousand jobs disappeared. When the proposed Chemical Banking–Chase Manhattan Corp. merger was announced in August 1995, estimates from the merging banks and from bank stock analysts predicted that as many as twelve thousand jobs might be lost.

Indeed, over the six years stretching from 1988 to 1994, New York state saw its total banking industry jobs decline from 184,300 in 1988 to 138,500 at the close of 1994, a decrease of nearly fifty thousand positions. In late 1994 BancOne Corp. announced nearly a 9 percent reduction in its work force (about forty-three hundred jobs) and the closing of approximately one hundred branch offices, these situated mainly in Illinois, Wisconsin, and

Ohio, following a decade of expansion in which that bank holding company acquired more than one hundred smaller banking firms. Moreover, when First Chicago and NBD committed to pursue a merger in June 1995, these banks agreed to reduce staff size by about seventeen hundred through attrition and layoffs, decreasing their combined work force from about 34,600 to about 32,900. Many authorities have predicted large-scale layoffs as interstate bank expansion proceeds and as automation replaces many teller and back-office positions. The key issue in many communities will be whether the fewer bank jobs available will be matched by greater employment opportunities in other industries. Clearly, there are no guarantees and no particularly reliable forecasts concerning future employment opportunities outside banking.

Branch Closings and Reduced Customer Convenience

To the extent that interstate banking firms increasingly penetrate the same markets, there will be more cases of overlapping branch offices that serve many of the same neighborhoods and communities. These duplications of both full-service and automated facilities offer tempting, often irresistible targets for bank management keenly interested in reducing costs. Indeed, the shutdown of bank branch offices has accelerated in recent years coincident with the interstate banking movement. Because most banks that participate in interstate mergers—both the acquired and acquiring banks—are relatively large and tend to have larger than average branch-office systems—the probability that merging interstate banks will have overlapping branch systems is relatively high.

This trend toward closing excess branch-office capacity helps explain why the U.S. Congress in recent years has imposed tougher requirements on banks proposing to close their service facilities, particularly in minority-dominated neighborhoods and in areas where branches are relatively scarce. The Riegle-Neal Interstate Banking Act of 1994 requires federal bank regulatory agencies to take into account the views of consumer groups and the financial needs of local areas when reviewing bankers' requests to close neighborhood office facilities. Moreover, it is not certain that interstate expansion will *necessarily* lead to a drastic decline in bank service facilities. As Federal Reserve Board economist Stephen A. Rhoades observes,

> the continuing increase in banking offices and checks written, even as the number of ATMs and ATM transactions grew dramatically, suggests that electronic banking in its present form has not eliminated the need for banking offices. Indeed, the local banking office may be a key way for banks to distinguish themselves from other financial-service providers and may have the potential to become a valuable retail platform for new banking products. Consequently, although banks must remain abreast of

and experiment with electronic banking, they may find it desirable to proceed cautiously with widespread office closings and, instead, develop a streamlined branch in the form of a mini-office. (1996, p. 29)

These conflicting trends, then, require special caution in predicting a decline or an increase in customer-convenient banking facilities, even as interstate banks expand their share of the industry's resources.

Survival Pressures on Small Banks and Their Stockholders

Many authorities have predicted the eventual demise of hundreds of small banks in the wake of banking industry consolidation. Some see cost pressures as the principal culprit in the disappearance of smaller banking firms, with larger banks allegedly being able to price their services lower as a result of economies of scale. Other authorities see small banks becoming victims of the loss of their customer base (i.e., the revenue side of the bank) as their clients are attracted away by the wider array of services and the more comprehensive advertising programs of larger, multistate banking companies.

The future for small banks may not be as bleak as the more pessimistic analysts suggest, however. More than thirty-two hundred new U.S. banks were chartered between 1980 and 1994, for example. This means that roughly half the potential industry-consolidating impact of the more than six thousand U.S. bank mergers occurring over the same time period was effectively erased by the creation of new banking firms. Moreover, larger correspondent banks in the nation's money centers have a long history of packaging their services in ways that smaller banks find more palatable. Thus, the smaller institutions may be able to continue to accommodate most of the service needs of their customers. Many bank customers prefer *quick decisions* (especially on loan applications) and *personalized service,* which smaller banks may be able to supply more efficiently. Small banks that focus their energies on *local* community needs, including the service demands of small businesses, individuals, and families, may still retain a significant competitive advantage over the largest interstate banking organizations, which tend to be more globally, rather than locally, focused.

A recent research study by Dr. Paul S. Calem (1994) of the Federal Reserve Bank of Philadelphia tends to support this last point. Calem's analysis of changes in state banking laws from the mid-1980s to early 1990s suggests that where states reduced or eliminated their branch banking laws, the number of small banks disappearing tended to rise significantly. This negative impact of more liberal in-state branching provisions on the small-bank population reflects the impact of in-state banking companies moving to a more efficient size once branching was allowed. Smaller, less efficient banks were then driven into mergers or forced to exit the industry because they could not match the low production costs of neighboring larger banks. Many smaller banks literally became more efficient by transforming themselves into branches of larger banks. However, once greater efficiency is achieved, there may be few additional efficiency gains available (at least within the limits of existing technology). Thus, merely passing a federal law to allow greater interstate banking and interstate branching activity is likely, in Calem's view, to have *few* effects on that status of small banks in the industry. Rather, Calem argues, nationwide branching will involve primarily consolidation among medium-size and larger banks, leaving the smallest industry units to seek out their own market niches where their services can remain profitable.

If so, this could be "good news" to those concerned about the availability of credit to the small business sector. Leonard Nakamura (1993), for example, finds that banking firms below $1 billion in asset size dominate the market for commercial loans under $1 million in size—the size loan most common among smaller business firms. In the same vein Paul Bauer and Brian Cromwell (1994) observe that small banks grant a disproportionally large share of loans to startup companies. Thus, if small banks continue to survive, the flow of credit to the small business sector may remain strong, though should a resale market for small business loans emerge, as called for by the Community Development and Regulatory Improvement Act of 1994, even the largest banks may find this market more attractive and expand their share of small business lending.

And, as Dr. Alan Greenspan (1994) noted during a speech in the wake of the huge floods along the Mississippi River in the mid-1990s, smaller community banks in the flooded areas led the effort to extend payment periods and offer lower loan rates to flooded businesses, farms, and homeowners so that business failure rates stayed low (and even declined in Iowa). Thus, small banks can offer more personalized services, acquire more easily and more profitably use local market knowledge, and extend to their customers easier access to officers of the bank—all features that most larger banks cannot easily replicate. Moreover, recent experience suggests that many newer product lines (such as mutual funds and security brokerage) can be offered by relatively small banks, often through joint ventures or franchising. Hundreds of small banks have continued to survive and perform well (even though recent changes in state and federal laws today leave few small banks actually sheltered from competition), indicating that these survivors from the ongoing acquisition wars either have become more efficient themselves (reaching the optimal size range for efficient operations largely by internal growth and cost-control measures) or have become niche banks that are well tailored to the special service and cost features of their local market areas. Most of these smaller institutions today are either rural banks or occupy uniquely favorable positions within urban and suburban markets.

Paul Calem (1994) forecasts several future trends under interstate banking:

1. Holding companies will consolidate their existing affiliates into unified branch office networks in the hope of providing greater customer convenience and achieving lower operating costs.

2. Smaller banks may merge with other small banks across state lines in order to achieve greater scale economies and lower operating costs.

Regardless, it doesn't seem likely to Calem that large numbers of small banks will be targeted for acquisition by large- and medium-size banks. Besides, small banks have ways of diversifying themselves against risk without taking part in consolidations and mergers. For example, a small bank can diversify its asset portfolio by selling loans or loan strips, by engaging in loan participations with other banks, or by expanding their security investments as a counterweight to a more risky loan portfolio. Currently there is no persuasive evidence that these forms of diversification are any less effective at reducing risk than are the geographic, portfolio, and product-line types of diversification often pursued by the largest banks in the industry. Calem argues that interstate expansion will be driven by the motives of:

1. geographic diversification to manage and control risk exposure

2. name recognition, which can help to attract new loan and deposit accounts

3. shedding excess capacity and increasing managerial efficiency

4. becoming organizations that are "too big to fail" (thus receiving government protection against ultimate collapse) while also gaining market power.

Federal Reserve Bank of Dallas economist Dr. Robert R. Moore (1995) has recently come to a somewhat different conclusion, however. Moore found that small banks (defined as the smallest one-third of a state's population of banks based on total assets) were generally losing market share during the 1980s and early 1990s. Moreover, these losses of market share by the smallest banks typically were occurring *before* most states lowered their barriers to branching and new entry, and that legislated liberalization of state bank entry laws did *not* accelerate the decline in market share that many smaller banks were experiencing. For example, Moore found that between 1982 and 1995 (first quarter), small banks' market share fell by more than ten percentage points in thirty-seven states. He argues that improvements in information and communications technology have reduced smaller banks' capacity to successfully fend off competition from larger banks and from nonbank competitors. Recent technological advances appear to have eroded somewhat the importance of the particular physical location chosen by a bank.

Loss of Local Influence over Bank Policies and Credit Decisions

Multinational corporations typically have great clout with most of the banks with whom they deal because so many banks are competing for the accounts of the largest corporations. Individuals and smaller firms generally do *not* possess significant market power, even in their own local areas. Fear of concentrated banking power has long been present in the United States precisely because banks offer vital financial services. As a bank grows, it normally becomes less and less dependent upon a single customer, a single local market area, or even a single industry. Thus, larger banks may become more insensitive to the complaints and service requests of smaller, highly localized customers.

One of the potential dangers associated with the spread of interstate banking, therefore, is the possible dwindling influence of smaller businesses and household customers in influencing when and where banking services will be provided and under what terms. The key question in this field focuses on the strength of competition in an environment of interstate banking and whether future competition will be sufficient to ensure a continuing supply of services to local customer groups.

A good example of the feeling of "helplessness" that some consumer groups have expressed in the wake of recent bank consolidations appeared when stockholders of Chemical Banking Corporation and Chase Manhattan voted in a shareholders' meeting in New York to proceed with their proposed combination, which was first announced on August 28, 1995. A group of protesters appeared at the meeting to object on grounds that the merger would, allegedly, offer "meager benefits" to low-income neighborhoods. The protesters cited the dangers associated with loss of jobs, higher service fees, and the erosion of community support that could result from the closing of neighborhood bank branch offices. In response, the managements of Chemical and Chase pledged themselves to provide loans to small businesses, nonprofit groups, and new home buyers. However, protesting consumer groups pointed to the checkered history of earlier bank mergers in not living up to the promises that had been made when these mergers were seeking regulatory approval (as noted, for example, by the National Community Reinvestment Coalition of Washington, D.C., representing more than five hundred community watch groups in the United States). This is especially of concern because of a perceived weakening in federal enforcement of the Community Reinvestment Act which requires banks and other covered lenders to make an "affirmative effort" to fully serve their local communities.

Loss of Federal Insurance Coverage on Some Deposits

Because of changes made in the U.S. deposit insurance system in recent years, insurance coverage has been reduced for some depositors, limited to essentially $100,000 per depositor per insured depository institution. In order to increase their insurance protection, many depositors have spread their deposits around among two or more different banks, each of which provides full insurance protection up to $100,000. As more and more local banks are absorbed into interstate systems, however, many businesses and wealthier depositors will find their insurance protection diminishing if two or more of their banks merge into a single corporation. In this case the Federal Deposit Insurance Corporation can pay no more than $100,000 in insurance claims to a single deposit owner even if his or her money is placed in several different branch offices of the same bank.

The severity of this problem is probably overstated. In the first place the great majority of depositors, including uninsured depositors, historically have recovered their funds when U.S. banks have failed. Moreover, the FDIC typically resolves most failures by finding another bank to purchase the failing institution's "clean" assets and assume *all* of its deposits. Finally, as the number of banks declines, nonbank depositories (such as savings and loans and credit unions), most of which also carry federal deposit insurance, offer additional relatively low-risk outlets for their depositors' funds.

WHY IT'S IMPORTANT TO ASSESS THE BENEFITS AND COSTS OF INTERSTATE BANKING NOW

This is an especially important time to assess the potential benefits and costs of the spread of interstate banking for a number of reasons. First, interstate banks do not *yet* dominate the American banking system. True, they are growing fast, but today they account for just over one-quarter of all domestic deposits. Second, federally mandated interstate branching cannot begin until the summer of 1997 unless individual states vote to begin that process earlier. If interstate banking is found to be damaging to the public welfare, there is still time to make adjustments in either state or federal laws or both or in the regulatory process for evaluating and approving interstate bank mergers and acquisitions in order to minimize the costs associated with this national banking trend.

Moreover, the history of interstate banking suggests a pattern of *gradual* change—a matter of years rather than months before major adjustments occur in the structure of banking nationally and globally—as acquisitions proceed slowly from one targeted region to another. Historically, most interstate companies have begun by expanding into neighboring states and then into adjacent regions before reaching further afield. If this pattern persists, as currently seems likely, there should still be opportunities to make midcourse adjustments in banking laws and regulations in order to optimize potential public benefits and minimize the costs associated with this major structural change now unfolding in American banking.

CHAPTER 5

The Research Evidence: What Is Known About Interstate Banking's Effects?

While serious research on the interstate banking phenomenon was virtually nonexistent before 1980, research in this field has increased significantly in recent years, particularly in the late 1980s and early 1990s. However, relative to most other controversial areas in banking, the volume of research focusing upon interstate banking still remains comparatively limited. Few issues can really be marked down as "decided," and the current body of evidence must be considered "thin" by conventional scientific standards. Certainly the restrictive nature of state and federal banking laws prior to passage of the 1994 Riegle-Neal Interstate Banking and Branching Efficiency Act in the United States helps to explain why so little has been resolved, research-wise, in the interstate banking field.

While looking at what research has been done in the interstate banking field, bear in mind that there are several different ways to measure the impact and influence of the interstate banking movement. For example, interstate banking may have a powerful impact on the internal organization and behavior of the individual banking firm but little impact outside the firm or upon the general public. Moreover, interstate banking might affect *some* performance dimensions of an individual bank, such as its profitability, but have almost no impact on other dimensions, such as its risk exposure. Similarly, interstate banking may or may not lead to improved bank service quality, service availability, operating efficiency, or depositor safety. Thus, it is *not* a simple matter to test what impact the growth of interstate banking might have on

Table 5.1
Possible Impacts of Interstate Expansion

Private Effects	*Public Effects*
Higher or lower profitability (including returns to shareholders, or rates of return on assets committed to the firm)	Enhanced or reduced competition (leading to a more competitive or less competitive marketplace)
Greater or lesser risk exposure (to the owners and employees of the individual banking firm)	Greater or lesser risk exposure (in terms of the safety of depositor funds and public confidence in the banking system)
Increased or reduced operating efficiency (in the use of productive resources [including management, staff, and capital])	Increased or decreased quality of banking services supplied to the public
	Larger or smaller quantity of banking services made available to the public
	Greater or lesser efficiency in the use of society's scarce resources (so that excessive amounts of the nation's resources may be committed to produce those banking services demanded by the public)
	Acceleration in the rate of economic growth and development, creating more opportunities for new jobs and new businesses

banks themselves and upon the public they serve. Those looking at recent research need to remember that interstate banking may have significant private effects on the individual firm, significant public effects on bank customers and on society as a whole, or neither significant public nor private effects. Some *possible* impacts of interstate expansion are shown in table 5.1.

THE POSSIBLE IMPACTS OF INTERSTATE BANKING UPON BANKING ORGANIZATIONS THEMSELVES

Impact on Bank Safety and Soundness (Is There a Geographic Diversification Effect?)

One of the most widely voiced claims in support of the spread of interstate banking is the belief that spreading out geographically into multiple markets

markets are significantly and positively correlated with each other or if new
markets targeted by an interstate company possess greater risk of return than
the markets where the interstate firm was previously rooted, the banking
company's overall risk exposure may not fall. Besides, banking organizations
face several other forms of risk—for example, operating risk in managing
and controlling labor and natural resources. Operating risk may increase in
a more diversified company due to the added complexities of trying to communicate with and manage people and resources over greater distances. Indeed, this form of risk may increase to such a degree that it offsets any
declines in financial or portfolio risk resulting from greater geographic diversity. Therefore, it is *not necessarily true* that the spread of interstate banking will reduce the overall risk exposure of either individual banks or of the
banking system as a whole. Risk may rise in some instances and fall in others.
The real-world risk effects of interstate bank expansion are a matter for
empirical investigation.

Is there any concrete evidence of a significant geographic diversification
effect in banking? A study by Nellie Liang and Stephen Rhoades (1988) of
the Federal Reserve Board examined approximately fifty-five hundred banks
over the 1976–85 period and uncovered a modest *inverse* relationship between bank earnings risk and the degree of geographic diversification
achieved. Banking firms operating in more than one local market appeared
to achieve lower risks to their net earnings compared to single-market banks.
As a partial offset, however, more geographically diverse banking organizations seemed to score lower average returns and to post somewhat lower
capital-to-asset ratios. Thus, a more geographically diverse banking company
may barter away at least some of its risk-reduction gains from entering multiple geographic markets by reducing its capital base relative to the risk-
exposed assets that it holds. Liang and Rhoades point out that expanding
geographically is really *not* the mirror image of the more familiar concept
of portfolio diversification involving financial assets due to the fact that,
unlike portfolio diversification, the achievement of greater geographic diversity may stimulate the management of an interstate firm to make changes
in organization (for example, to network more branches in order to overcome distance problems) that influence the company's overall risk exposure.
In summary, geographic diversification may be a two-edged sword, reducing
bank earnings risk but increasing other dimensions of bank risk exposure.

Only a handful of studies have looked at the correlation of returns among
large numbers of banks in several different states. One of the most recent is an
analysis of Pacific Coast and Rocky Mountain states belonging to the Twelfth
Federal Reserve District (which includes Alaska, Arizona, California, Hawaii,
Idaho, Nevada, Oregon, Utah, and Washington) by economist Dr. Mark Levonian (1994). Levonian correlated the asset returns for thirty-six possible
pairings of the foregoing states covering the 1985–93 period.[1] Only banks
with less than $300 million in aggregate assets were included in the study be-
cause these smaller institutions were presumed to be more likely to serve lo-

calized markets rather than whole regions encompassing more than one state or even the nation as a whole. Levonian found only *three* western state pairings in which the asset return correlations were negative and statistically significant, indicating the greatest potential for at least some geographic diversification benefits from combining banks in these particular states within the same organization. The negatively correlated state pairings involved banks in Arizona versus California, Hawaii versus Utah, and Hawaii versus Oregon.

Interestingly enough, the Bank of America and First Interstate Banks (later merged with Wells Fargo), both headquartered in California, have entered Arizona already, while Bank of America has expanded into both Oregon and Hawaii. Overall, twenty-one combinations of pairs of these western states had either negative or positive, but near zero correlations in earnings, measured by their banks' asset returns. In contrast, just fifteen West Coast and Rocky Mountain state combinations were positively correlated at a statistically significant level. Positively correlated returns that are high enough to be statistically significant would appear to offer relatively little in geographic diversification benefits but may still make good economic sense if they represent growing and profitable bank marketing opportunities.

One word of caution: the variance of earnings may be higher in some states than in others, perhaps making the entering bank *more*, not less, risky as a result of greater geographic diversification. For example, Levonian found that Alaska and Arizona have comparatively high-variance asset returns, while Oregon, Washington, and California tend to have more stable returns. In these instances geographic diversification may be unable to offset the additional volatility that comes from entering a high earnings-variance state. Levonian also found that earnings risk reduction appeared to come primarily from interest income on loans and loan-loss provisions, which are *not* highly correlated across states and, in a few cases, display negative correlations.[2]

Several of Levonian's conclusions for the Pacific and Rocky Mountain states appear to be consistent with the bank earnings correlations obtained by the present author for the whole United States. In this study (Rose, 1995) the author formed four different classes of banks based on their total assets for all years over the 1985–93 period for every state in the union and the District of Columbia. The bank size classes included all billion-dollar-plus banks in each state, all banks in the $100 million to $1 billion range, all banks with assets totaling less than $100 million, and, finally, a class with all U.S. insured banks notwithstanding their size.

Tables 5.2 and 5.3 indicate some of the greatest and smallest state-by-state correlations for returns on bank assets. Note an absence of significant return correlations bearing negative signs when bank size was *not* taken into account—that is, when banks were not differentiated by size group. For the biggest U.S. banking firms, there were few groups of states with negative correlations of their asset returns. It should be noted, though, that 220 pairs of states reported nonsignificant negative correlations among the asset returns of the biggest U.S. banking firms.

Table 5.2
States Reporting the Most Negative Intercorrelations of Bank Asset Returns with Other States, 1985–93

All FDIC-Insured Banks		Banks with Assets over $1 Billion		Banks with Assets $100 to $1 Billion		Banks with Assets under $100 Million	
Hawaii/ Vermont	-0.623	Maryland/ Montana	-0.626	Connecticut/ Idaho	-0.940*	Hawaii/ South Carolina	-0.904*
Maine/ Wyoming	-0.605	Hawaii/ Virginia	-0.582	Connecticut/ Wyoming	-0.830*	Idaho/ Tennessee	-0.890*
Vermont/ Washington	-0.590	Hawaii/ New Jersey	-0.579	Delaware/ Vermont	-0.818*	Arkansas/ Delaware	-0.885*
Connecticut/ Wyoming	-0.583	Hawaii/ Kansas	-0.568	Idaho/ New Jersey	-0.815*	Arkansas/ Maryland	-0.881*
Oklahoma/ Vermont	-0.579	Hawaii/ Maryland	-0.565	Delaware/ New York	-0.813*	Illinois/ Pennsylvania	-0.873*
California/ Maryland	-0.578	D.C./ Oklahoma	-0.543	Connecticut/ Montana	-0.809*	Arkansas/ South Carolina	-0.872*
D.C./ Washington	-0.567	California/ New Mexico	-0.536	Connecticut/ Oregon	-0.807*	California/ South Carolina	-0.870*
California/ Connecticut	-0.555	California/ Maryland	-0.535	New York/ Wyoming	-0.779*	Connecticut/ Idaho	-0.864*
D.C./ Oklahoma	-0.553	New Mexico/ Washington	-0.528	Connecticut/ Michigan	-0.764*	Delaware/ Virginia	-0.862*
Maine/ Montana	-0.550	Arizona/ Hawaii	-0.500	New York/ Oregon	-0.761*	Kansas/ Vermont	-0.857*
Hawaii/ New Jersey	-0.550	Alaska/ Iowa	-0.499	California/ Kentucky	-0.755*	Arkansas/ Indiana	-0.857*

Connecticut/ Montana	-0.542	Michigan/ Montana	-0.493	California/ Texas	-0.753*	Arkansas/ South Carolina	-0.854
Michigan/ Vermont	-0.541	D.C./ Idaho	-0.492	Montana/ New York	-0.736	Alabama/ Hawaii	-0.852*
Maine/ Washington	-0.539	D.C./ South Dakota	-0.485	Idaho/ Massachusetts	-0.735	Arizona/ South Carolina	-0.847*
Montana/ Vermont	-0.538	Maryland/ Oregon	-0.481	New Jersey/ Wyoming	-0.725	Indiana/ Iowa	-0.852*
Nebraska/ Vermont	-0.536	Montana/ Vermont	-0.477	California/ Nebraska	-0.720	Alabama/ Hawaii	-0.852*
D.C./ Montana	-0.535	New Mexico/ Oklahoma	-0.469	Montana/ New Jersey	-0.712	Colorado/ Pennsylvania	-0.840*
Hawaii/ Virginia	-0.535	New Mexico/ Oklahoma	-0.468	California/ Washington	-0.711	Hawaii/ Indiana	-0.840*
Maine/ Oklahoma	-0.529	Maine/ Washington	-0.468	New York/ Oklahoma	-0.709	Iowa/ South Carolina	-0.839*
Idaho/ Maine	-0.522	Connecticut/ Washington	-0.462	California/ Tennessee	-0.706	Delaware/ Hawaii	-0.834*

Notes:

Based on FDIC data supplied by insured banks.

*Indicates a correlation coefficient statistically significant at least at the 0.05 risk level.

Source: Study by the author covering the 1985–93 period.

Table 5.3
States Reporting the Most Positive Intercorrelations of Bank Asset Returns with Other States, 1985–93

All FDIC-Insured Banks		Banks with Assets over $1 Billion		Banks with Assets $100 to $1 Billion		Banks with Assets under $100 Million	
Arkansas/ South Dakota	0.989*	Delaware/ West Virginia	0.997*	D.C./ Vermont	0.960*	Kansas/ West Virginia	0.939*
Connecticut/ New Jersey	0.987*	Nebraska/ Vermont	0.996*	Massachusetts/ New Jersey	0.959*	Connecticut/ Vermont	0.929*
Florida/ New Hampshire	0.986*	Arizona/ Arkansas	0.995*	Oklahoma/ Oregon	0.958*	Arizona/ D.C.	0.924*
Iowa/ South Dakota	0.983*	Tennessee/ Vermont	0.995*	Montana/ Oregon	0.954*	Arkansas/ Arizona	0.914*
Idaho/ Iowa	0.980*	Arkansas/ Wyoming	0.995*	Ohio/ Wisconsin	0.953*	Arkansas/ Virginia	0.909*
Florida/ Kentucky	0.979*	Mississippi/ New Hampshire	0.994*	Louisiana/ Oregon	0.953*	D.C./ Iowa	0.909*
Florida/ Tennessee	0.978*	Colorado/ Wyoming	0.993*	Maryland/ South Dakota	0.953*	Arkansas/ D.C.	0.901*
Indiana/ Ohio	0.975*	Louisiana/ West Virginia	0.993*	Illinois/ Ohio	0.952*	Arizona/ Iowa	0.894*
Idaho/ South Dakota	0.972*	Florida/ New Hampshire	0.992*	Texas/ Utah	0.950*	Florida/ Wisconsin	0.891*
Kansas/ Michigan	0.971*	New Hampshire/ New Jersey	0.991*	Arkansas/ South Dakota	0.949*	Hawaii/ Iowa	0.887*
Idaho/ Nebraska	0.968*	Connecticut/ New Mexico	0.991*	Indiana/ Tennessee	0.948*	D.C./ Florida	0.885*
Hawaii/ Idaho	0.968*	Vermont/ Wyoming	0.990*			Connecticut/ Tennessee	0.884*
Maryland/ Massachusetts	0.965*	Connecticut/ New Hampshire	0.990*			Hawaii/ Virginia	0.883*
		Nebraska/ Wyoming	0.990*			Arizona/ Florida	0.882*
		Missouri/ West Virginia	0.989*			California/ Virginia	0.871*

Notes:
Based on FDIC data supplied by insured banks.
*Indicates a correlation coefficient statistically significant at least at the 0.05 risk level.

Source: Study by the author covering the 1985–93 period.

For smaller-size banks, however, there were more opportunities for real geographic diversification. For example, across states where there were banks in the middle and smaller asset size ranges, possibilities existed for matching groups of acquired banks bearing low or even negatively correlated earnings. Examples included such sets of states as California and Colorado; Connecticut and Idaho; North Dakota and Texas; and Maine and Utah. Nevertheless, overall there were few pairs of states with inverse earnings correlations.

Overwhelmingly, bank earnings display direct relationships rather than indirect (negative) relationships. When asset returns are rising in neighboring states, they also generally go up in a bank's home state as well. This seems to happen regardless of bank size. (See table 5.3 for examples of state pairs with direct return correlations.) Among the most prominent significantly positive earnings correlations were such groups of states as Arkansas and South Dakota; Connecticut and New Jersey; Delaware and West Virginia; and Washington, D.C. and Vermont. Often, these are difficult relationships to explain because, on the surface at least, some of these latter state pairings, despite their highly correlated bank earnings records, would seem to present widely different economic and demographic profiles.

The correlations shown in tables 5.2 and 5.3 suggest that the range of states offering real diversification potential is limited. This last observation gives rise to an interesting question: where does the direct (positive) relationship between bank earnings in one state versus all other states come from? Note that a bank's net after-tax income is derived from the following elements: (a) interest and fee income on loans and securities less interest expense on deposits and other borrowed funds; (b) noninterest service fee income less salaries and other noninterest expenses; (c) loan-loss provision expense; (d) securities gains or losses; (e) extraordinary income or expense items; and (f) any tax obligations incurred. When these various net-earnings elements were examined, the strongest state-by-state relationships lay on the funding side of bank activities. Interest costs paid out to attract funds showed the highest direct relationships among banks headquartered in different states and regions of the nation. Considering all possible combinations of two-state banking affiliations that could be calculated among the fifty states and the District of Columbia, only slightly more than 15 percent of these correlations of bank interest expenses (divided by total assets) were *not* statistically significant (at the 5 percent significance level) in the positive direction, and less than 2 percent of all possible state-by-state interest expense correlations were negative (none significantly so).

This finding is consistent with the notion that deregulation of the American banking sector, which began (as shown in chapter 3) during the 1980s, has welded what used to be thousands of localized savings markets into a national, even international, market for savings. The rapid development of the money market mutual fund from 1972 onward has made it easy for small savers in any local area to send in a check, wire funds, or automatically draft their checking accounts and contribute to money market share accounts hundreds, if not thousands, of miles away. If this observation is true, it means that bankers cannot look primarily at their deposit customers as a principal source of the risk-reducing benefits of geographic diversity.

If they are to achieve real diversity through a variety of market presences, U.S. bankers must look to their sources of cash inflow from loans and other earning assets as the basis for a strategy of geographic expansion. It is interesting, for example, to compare the state-by-state correlations for bank loan income versus the state-by-state correlations for interest expense (also relative to total assets) for each size group of banks. For example, among the smallest banks (those with less than $100 million in assets) fifty-one pairs of state-by-state ratios of loan interest income to total assets were negatively related, but just twenty-four of the state-by-state interest expense totals were negatively correlated (none significantly so). More than one thousand state pairs of interest costs were positively and significantly (at the 5 percent risk level) correlated among the small banks. For medium ($100 million- to $1 billion-size) banks, forty-four pairs of state-by-state loan revenues were negatively correlated, while there were *no* negatively correlated state pairs for the interest cost-to-assets ratio. All but fifty-two of the state-by-state interest expense correlations were positively significant at the 5 percent risk level among the medium-size banks. Thus, diversification from interstate expansion and growth seems to lie largely in a bank's credit portfolio, especially if states in different regions can be brought together.

Of course, the range of suitable states to achieve real earnings diversification benefits may be even narrower if those states displaying high return variances are taken into account. Entering some states possessing negative or low positive earnings correlations may still result in more risky bank returns, because the variance of returns in those states lies well above the industry average.

For example, the top ten U.S. states in terms of the variance of asset returns over the 1985–93 period are shown in table 5.4. Notice that the particular asset size group in which a bank is found plays an important role in shaping relative bank return variances among the states. Alaska ranked highest in asset return variance among all states' banks over the 1985–93 period, whereas small and medium banks from Alabama, the District of Columbia, Wisconsin, and New Hampshire ranked highest in those particular asset size groups. If interstate acquiring firms choose acquired banks with above-average return variances and the acquired institutions represent a substantial proportion of the total assets of the postacquisition consolidated banking firm, then the overall return variance of the interstate acquiring organization could increase, canceling out any geographic diversification benefits achieved by expanding across state lines.

Some states have reported exceptionally high average (mean) bank return levels that may justify taking on some degree of added risk. Table 5.5 pres-

Table 5.4
States Reporting the Highest Bank Return Variances, 1985–93 (U.S.-insured commercial banks, ROA variance)

All FDIC-Insured Banks		Banks with Assets Over $1 Billion		Banks with Assets of $100 Million to $1 Billion		Banks with Assets Under $100 Million	
Alaska	.487	Alaska	1.083	Washington, D.C.	.551	Alabama	.681
Washington, D.C.	.205	New Hampshire	.464	New Hampshire	.180	Wisconsin	.381
New Hampshire	.167	Washington, D.C.	.176	Alaska	.126	Nebraska	.266
Connecticut	.116	Texas	.118	Delaware	.120	Delaware	.220
Texas	.069	Connecticut	.118	Wyoming	.097	Minnesota	.197
Nevada	.068	South Dakota	.115	Connecticut	.096	Iowa	.162
South Dakota	.061	Oklahoma	.101	Massachusetts	.089	North Dakota	.132
Oklahoma	.058	Nevada	.083	Oklahoma	.067	Alaska	.129
Delaware	.052	Louisiana	.065	Louisiana	.057	Kansas	.094
New Jersey	.052	New Jersey	.061	Texas	.053	Rhode Island	.079

Source: Study by the author covering the 1985–93 period.

ents the top ten states in terms of mean bank asset returns (average for 1985 through 1993).

Once again, *bank size* emerges as an important factor. States that rank among the highest in large-bank mean asset returns do not necessarily display exceptional earnings averages among their small and medium banks. Among smaller banking institutions the states of Alabama, Pennsylvania, Washington, and Indiana ranked at the top in mean asset returns during the 1985–93 period, while Delaware and South Dakota dominated the mean returns list for medium-size banks.

What happens to these conclusions if states in a given region are combined and one region is compared against another? Because the particular regional boundaries used may matter, the author tested three different regional concepts as viewed by the Federal Reserve System (i.e., Federal Reserve districts) and as viewed by two federal government departments—the U.S. Department of Commerce and the U.S. Census. As the figures given in tables 5.6 and 5.7 reveal, classifying banking activity by region tends to intensify the strong direct relationships between bank earnings in one locale versus another. Over time, regional disparities in bank returns do not appear to be hugely different, though there have been periods when one region or another (e.g., New England and the Southwest during the 1980s) has experienced substantial losses in bank earnings and numerous bank failures. The tendency for all regions to display similar bank-earnings tracks suggests that bankers would be better off to analyze acquisition targets at the state or local level and not at the regional level. If there is any capacity for regional diversification, the figures in tables 5.6 and 5.7 argue that widely dispersed

Table 5.5
States Reporting the Highest Mean Asset Returns, 1985–93

All FDIC-Insured Banks		Banks with Assets Over $1 Billion		Banks with Assets of $100 Million to $1 Billion		Banks with Assets Under $100 Million	
South Dakota	2.26%	South Dakota	2.86%	Delaware	1.97%	Alabama	1.97%
Nevada	1.82	Nevada	2.07	South Dakota	1.52	Pennsylvania	1.07
Delaware	1.73	Delaware	1.73	Georgia	1.18	Washington	1.04
Alabama	1.11	New Hampshire	1.55	Washington	1.16	Indiana	1.04
West Virginia	1.10	Iowa	1.30	North Carolina	1.13	South Carolina	1.03
Ohio	1.08	Arkansas	1.10	West Virginia	1.11	Texas	0.97
Washington	1.01	Montana	1.18	Illinois	1.10	Arkansas	0.96
Hawaii	1.00	Ohio	1.10	Virginia	1.10	Minnesota	0.96
Wisconsin	0.99	West Virginia	1.09	Alabama	1.09	Delaware	0.94
Oregon	0.98	Wyoming	1.07	Wisconsin	1.07	Ohio	0.90

Source: Study by the author covering 1985–93 period.

regional groups may provide the strongest diversification impact—for example, combining banks situated along the Pacific Rim (including the states of Alaska, California, Hawaii, Oregon, and Washington) with banks headquartered in the New England region (Connecticut, Maine, Massachusetts, New Hampshire, Rhode Island, and Vermont) or banks along the U.S. West Coast with banks in the Upper Midwest or those situated in the New York, New Jersey, and Pennsylvania (Atlantic) region. However, not all states in these widely separated regions are equally attractive. That is why a state-by-state analysis is preferable to only a broad regional view of U.S. banking markets.

Recently the author has taken the state-by-state diversification analysis a step further by analyzing the interstate diversification actually achieved by eighty-four large U.S. bank holding companies over the 1980–92 period. Rose (1996b) used multiple measures of banking risk, including the probability of insolvency, coefficient of income variation, and measures of liquidity, credit, and capital risk as well as the standard deviations of ROE and ROA. The study also included measures of bank operating efficiency and employee productivity and sought to explain both risk and efficiency indicators with variables representing the degree of interstate geographic diversity, asset portfolio composition, capital mix, and the number of banks acquired. The study found that diversification *across state lines was frequently risk increasing until certain threshold levels were reached.* Above these "geographic diversity thresholds" (generally, once affiliates were acquired by an interstate company in four or more states and in at least two distinct geographic regions), significant reductions in risk exposure and operating costs often occurred. However, the impact of geographic diversification varied

Table 5.6

Highest and Lowest Regional U.S.-Insured Bank Return (ROA) Correlations, 1985–93 (Regions defined by the U.S. Department of Commerce)

Regions	Correlations of the Different Regions Listed in the Far Left Column with Other U.S. Regions:							
	All FDIC-Insured Banks		Banks with Assets Over $1 Billion		Banks with Assets of $100 Million to $1 Billion		Banks with Assets under $100 Million	
Atlantic States	Great Lakes	0.890*	Great Lakes	0.912*	New England	0.868*	Great Lakes	0.531
	New England	0.382	New England	0.479	Far West	-0.329	Far West	-0.349
Great Lakes States	Atlantic	0.890*	Southwest	0.920*	Plains	0.972*	Atlantic	0.531
	New England	0.115	New England	0.139	Far West	-0.420*	Far West	-0.579
Plains States	Rocky Mountain	0.965*	Rocky Mountain	0.958*	Southeast	0.972*	Southeast	0.907*
	New England	-0.046	New England	0.163	Far West	-0.352	Great Lakes	-0.322
Southeast States	New England	0.756*	New England	0.841*	Plains	0.972*	Plains	0.907*
	Far West	0.242	Far West	0.109	Far West	-0.434	Great Lakes	-0.457
Rocky Mountain States	Plains	0.796*	Plains	0.958*	Southwest	0.940*	Southwest	0.958*
	New England	0.113	New England	0.287	Far West	-0.454	Great Lakes	0.241
Far West States	Great Lakes	0.796*	Plains	0.820*	Southwest	-0.287	Southeast	0.874*
	New England	-0.401	New England	-0.271	New England	-0.487	Great Lakes	-0.579
New England States	Southeast	0.756*	Southeast	0.841*	Atlantic	0.868*	Southwest	0.817*
	Plains	-0.046	Far West	-0.271	Far West	-0.487	Great Lakes	-0.063

Note:

*Indicates a statistically significant correlation at the 0.05 risk level.

Source: Study by the author covering the 1985–93 period.

Table 5.7
Highest and Lowest Regional U.S.-Insured Bank Return (ROA) Correlations, 1985–93 (Regions defined by the U.S. Bureau of the Census)

Regions	Correlations of the Regions Listed in the Far Left Column with Other U.S. Regions:							
	All FDIC-Insured Banks		Banks with Assets over $1 Billion		Banks with Assets of $100 Million to $1 Billion		Banks with Assets under $100 Million	
New England States	East South Central	.837*	East South Central	.900*	Mid-Atlantic	0.919*	East North Central	0.874*
	Pacific	-0.431	Pacific	-0.296	Pacific	-0.489	Mid-Atlantic	-0.434
Mid-Atlantic States	East North Central	0.865*	East North Central	0.903*	New England	0.919*	Pacific	0.406
	New England	0.443	New England	0.466	West South Central	-0.437	West South Central	-0.486
East North Central States	Mountain	.887*	West North Central	0.905*	East North Central	0.972*	West South Central	0.890*
	New England	0.115	New England	0.139	Pacific	-0.453	Mid-Atlantic	-0.293
West North Central States	Mountain	0.897*	East North Central	0.905*	East North Central	0.972*	New England	0.793
	New England	-0.046	New England	0.139	Pacific	-0.390	East South Central	0.055
South Atlantic States	East South Central	0.977*	East South Central	0.939*	East South Central	0.983*	West North Central	0.575
	Pacific	0.201	Pacific	0.295	Pacific	-0.588	East South Central	-0.464
East South Central States	South Atlantic	0.977*	South Atlantic	.939*	South Atlantic	0.983*	West South Central	0.576
	Pacific	0.099	Pacific	0.108	Pacific	-0.630	East South Central	-0.464

West South Central States	West North Central	0.890*	East North Central	0.895*	Mountain	0.943*	East North Central	0.890*
	New England	-0.065	New England	0.005	Mid Atlantic	-0.437	Mid-Atlantic	-0.486
Mountain States	West North Central	0.897*	South Atlantic Pacific	0.934*	West South Central	0.943*	West North Central	0.621
	New England	0.347		0.476	Pacific	-0.356	Pacific	-0.073
Pacific States	East North Central	0.783*	West South Central	0.832*	Mid-Atlantic East South	-0.257	East South Central	0.572
	East South Central	0.099	New England	-0.296	Central	-0.630	New England	-0.179

Note:
*Indicates the correlation coefficient is statistically significant at least at the 0.05 risk level.

Source: Study by the author covering the 1985–93 period.

widely with the particular risk measure and geographic diversification measure employed.

Clearly, the issue of geographic diversification and risk reduction in banking is a complex one with conflicting features. Overall, the potential for geographically related risk reduction appears to be relatively small—of a secondary, not primary, order of magnitude and importance. Banking organizations expanding across state lines with geographic diversification as the sole managerial objective are likely to be disappointed. Other economic or financial objectives must be carefully considered before the decision is made to cross state lines and build a more geographically diverse banking entity. Moreover, as a recent study by Faulhaber (1995) shows, large banks (over $1 billion in assets) tend to take on greater risk in their operations.

OTHER FACTORS THAT MAY DRIVE INTERSTATE BANK EXPANSION

The research literature on interstate banking has recently begun to seriously grapple with the central issue: *what really motivates a banking firm to pursue interstate expansion?* If interstate banking companies don't possess a significant economic or financial advantage over noninterstate banking firms in at least *one* dimension of their performance, then how can the interstate movement be expected to grow? If, for example, geographic diversification potential is so small and limited, what else must be driving the trend toward interstate banking?

The author carried out two studies in the late 1980s (see Rose 1989a, b) attempting to detect the motives for interstate expansion by examining the preacquisition performance of both interstate acquirers and their target acquired banking firms relative to banking companies not involved in interstate expansion. These studies found that interstate firms were more heavily dependent upon so-called core deposits (smaller demand and time accounts with relatively low interest-rate elasticity) and displayed higher noninterest operating expenses and lower earnings margins than comparably sized noninterstate banking companies, suggesting that interstate-bound banks seek lower cost and more stable deposits, economies of scale, and improved margins when they cross state lines.

Looking at the banks acquired across state boundaries during the 1980–87 period the author found that, on average, interstate acquisition targets were subpar in their rates of return on assets and equity capital, in production efficiency, and in controlling loan losses. These important performance deficiencies suggested that, in the 1980s at least, interstate companies focused primarily on *potential performance gains* from cross-border acquisitions after new management came in, rather than buying top-performing institutions that would be priced higher in an efficient market. Moreover, a strategy focused on buying banks that are already performing well might offer little room for future performance gains that acquiring companies' management might be able to point to as an indicator of their success.

Some bank researchers have focused upon *bank size* as the key driving force behind recent interstate acquisitions. Allegedly, banks that expand geographically can achieve greater overall operating size than other banks and, therefore, may enjoy size-related gains in operating efficiency, revenue productivity, or risk reduction. For example, Federal Reserve economists Patrick McAllister and Douglas McManus (1992) correlated bank size over the 1984–90 period with the mean returns and return variability from bank loan portfolios of varying size reaching up to the largest banks who reported loan portfolios approaching $10 billion in size. They found what appeared to be positive returns to scale in lending and potential real gains from loan portfolio diversification. As loan portfolios expanded the correlations among loan defaults and loan returns tended to decline, decreasing the risk of bank insolvency. McAllister and McManus see powerful implications for public policy in their findings, which they view as supporting a more open interstate merger policy as a way to lower overall bank risk and, in the long run, improve the stability and profitability of U.S. banking companies.

Unfortunately, this is a field where positive research findings are often contradicted by negative research findings. In response to the same issue— do interstate companies possess significant long-run economic and financial advantages that give them an edge over other types of banking companies?— two academic researchers, Lawrence Goldberg and Gerald Hanweck (1988), find few affirmative economic reasons to support interstate banking. These authors tracked the market shares, profitability, and growth of a relatively small group of banking companies that had already crossed state lines in the decades prior to passage of the Bank Holding Company Act of 1956, which, as seen in chapter 2, prohibited cross-border controlling interests in out-of-state bank stock by holding companies unless the states to be entered specifically approved these acquisitions. By following the profitability and growth of these grandfathered interstate banking companies over about a decade and a half, these researchers found *no* convincing evidence of higher average profitability among interstate banks compared to banking organizations housed within a single state.

In fact, these earliest interstate banking companies reported a *declining* share of all deposits compared to their intrastate competitors. Goldberg and Hanweck concluded that long-run competition probably eradicated any organizational benefits that interstate companies may have possessed over non-interstate banking firms when they first launched their cross-border acquisition strategies. Similar findings have been recorded by J. T. Rose and J. D. Wolken (1990), who studied the effects of banks becoming affiliated with a geographically diversified bank holding company. The acquired institutions generally did *not* improve their market shares relative to independent competitors.

In a more recent inquiry, Federal Reserve Bank of New York economist William Lee (1993) looked for relationships between stock values, rates of return, and the degree of geographic diversity achieved by publicly traded holding companies. He observed a direct (positive) relationship between the level of geographic diversity achieved and organizational price-earnings (P/E) ratios. Banking companies represented in a wider array of local markets tended to have higher stock price to earnings ratios. However, holding-company bond ratings seemed to be somewhat negatively related to geographic diversity. Lee concluded that interstate companies face greater opportunities for high returns as they diversify geographically, but they also encounter increased risks in their daily operations as more and more "unfamiliar markets" are entered. Thus, there may be costs in the form of greater risk associated with moving across state lines, but these costs may be wholly or partially offset by increasing stock prices for the companies involved.

Searching for greater returns to stockholders when banks expand across state lines is a common thread among a substantial number of recent research studies. Because forty-nine of fifty states changed their banking laws during the 1980s and early 1990s, several recent studies have attempted to determine if bank stock prices were influenced by these changes in interstate banking laws. As Marcus (1984) has found, changes in laws and regulations, either at the state level or the federal level, affect the market's valuation of a bank charter—which is simply an option, limited in supply by government regulation, to perform the business of banking and thereby gain access to future banking profits. It might be supposed that any state that enacts new interstate banking legislation would do so primarily to benefit banks and, thereby, enhance the market value of bank charters for those banking companies affected by the change in law. However, if banking laws are liberalized to allow greater latitude for interstate banking, the result for at least some banks may be greater *competition*, which would tend to reduce bank profitability, increase earnings risk, and possibly reduce the stock prices of the banks affected.

Which way have stock prices and bank earnings gone as a result of recent changes in interstate banking legislation? One study by Black, Fields, and Schweitzer (1990) explored the responses of fifty-one banking firms headquartered in seventeen states that changed their interstate banking laws during the 1980s. In this case, regional banking companies experienced positively significant gains in stock values as a result of the new interstate rules, presumably because the regional companies involved gained additional opportunities for revenue expansion (and, possibly, greater economies of scale or scope) as legal entry barriers were lowered. In contrast, the nation's largest money-center banks generally lost value (but not significantly so) in the wake of the changes in state laws studied by Black, Fields, and Schweitzer, perhaps because the new expansion powers would allow regional companies to pose stronger competition for money-center banks.

However, not all the evidence on the impact of interstate banking laws is in agreement. A more recent study by Goldberg, Hanweck, and Sugure (1992) explored the bank valuation outcomes for 191 banking firms resulting from thirty-five state legislative changes. This research study found *negative* returns, on average, for those banking companies residing in the states where these legislative changes occurred, perhaps because capital-market investors anticipated greater competition for in-state banks as legal entry barriers fell. However, banks in neighboring states that would be allowed to enter new territory as a result of these state-law changes seemed to gain from the announcement of the new cross-border banking legislation.

Several other recent studies have looked for possible gains in bank stock values, profitability, or other performance dimensions in the wake of interstate mergers or acquisitions. For example, positive shareholder gains from interstate expansion were found by M. Millon-Cornett teamed, first, with S. De (1991) and then with H. Tehranian (1992). The first of these two research studies observed excess returns from interstate mergers, 1982–86, received by the shareholders of *both* interstate acquirers and the acquired banking companies, especially when failing banks were not involved in the merger and where state laws offered some protection against outside entry from other states. The positive returns were *not* equally distributed, however, as acquired stockholders received excess returns of +6.08 percent, while shareholders for the interstate acquiring institutions scored a much less impressive +0.65 percent average excess return.

Employing a slightly expanded sample, Millon-Cornett and Tehranian (1992) targeted large-bank mergers and acquisitions between 1982 and 1987. These researchers found that the merged companies generally did better than otherwise comparable institutions—a cross-section of the industry in cash-flow returns; employee productivity; the growth of assets, deposits, and loans; and the control of problem loans. In a study covering part of the same period (1985–87) as the Millon-Cornett-Tehranian study, K. Spong and J. D. Shoenhair (1992) observed some of the same postmerger benefits that the former researchers identified, particularly in the difficult managerial areas of controlling operating costs and in securing reasonably adequate returns for bank stockholders.

Unfortunately, the research findings regarding the benefits of large bank acquisitions, particularly interstate mergers, are *not* all positive. For example, J. Trifts and K. Scanlon (1987) found that, while the stockholders of target banking firms generally scored gains following their acquisition, this was not usually true for the banking companies pursuing these acquisition targets. A possible exception centered around the relative size of acquisitions, where bigger interstate banking acquisitions appeared to have a greater chance of scoring excess earnings when access to more promising new markets was the result of a merger or holding company acquisition. Continuing in the same general theme, J. Born, R. Eisenbeis, and R. Harris (1988) uncovered *no* persistent earnings bonus in the period immediately before or after bank expansion plans (i.e., mergers or new entry) were announced. Born et. al. concluded that potential gains by acquiring firm shareholders have largely been distributed vis-à-vis competition to the stockholders of acquired firms or, perhaps, are consumed by the non-earnings-related goals of the acquiring institutions.

Actually, the financial success or lack of success of an interstate banking merger may depend upon how much overlapping in facilities the merging institutions have. For example, a study from the Federal Reserve Bank of Dallas by Thomas Siems (1996) finds that megamergers occurring in the United States in 1995 resulted in higher returns when the merging banking firms had more office overlaps—that is, more duplications in the locations of their service facilities, which permitted them to close or downsize at least some overlapping offices.

Of 19 largest bank mergers investigated by Seims (including Fleet Financial Group's acquisition of Shawnut National, First Union Corp.'s merger with First Fidelity Bancorp, Bank of Boston's purchase of BayBank, Chemical's acquisition of Chase Manhattan Corp., and Wells Fargo's acquisition of First Interstate) the five big mergers with the greatest proportion of overlapping office facilities scored significant positive abnormal returns for their stockholders. In contrast, the remainder of these 19 super-size mergers resulted in *negative* abnormal stock returns. Interestingly enough, Siems (1996) also finds that apparent increases in market power (measured by increased concentration) following a merger did *not* result in significant positive abnormal returns for stockholders and finds evidence as well that the managements of acquirers tended to benefit more than their shareholders from these largest bank mergers. Moreover, he observes that acquiring banks tended to overbid for their acquisition-targeted banks, resulting in more cases of negative, rather than positive, stockholder returns.

In summary, interstate banking companies reaching across state lines have enjoyed highly mixed outcomes and questionable gains for the companies themselves, according to recent research. Interstate expansion does *not* guarantee success in risk-adjusted returns. Shareholders of acquired firms appear to score some excess returns, but the evidence is much less clear as to how well or poorly stockholders belonging to acquiring interstate banking firms fare in the wake of cross-border mergers and acquisitions. Some large multistate institutions fall far short of their earnings and risk management goals, which helps to explain why many noninterstate banking firms continue to thrive and prosper. It has not yet been demonstrated convincingly that interstate banks possess significant economic or financial advantages over non-interstate-oriented banks.

Table 5.8
Shares of Domestic Commercial Banking Assets Held by the Largest Banking Organizations Operating in the United States, 1980–95

Year	Top 5	Top 10	Top 25	Top 50	Top 100
1980	13.5	21.6	33.1	41.6	51.4
1981	13.2	21.1	33.2	41.6	51.6
1982	13.7	21.8	34.2	43.0	53.6
1983	13.2	21.0	34.0	43.3	54.3
1984	13.0	20.4	33.3	43.7	55.4
1985	12.8	20.4	33.2	45.8	57.9
1986	12.7	20.2	34.1	47.3	60.4
1987	12.6	19.9	34.8	48.5	61.9
1988	12.8	20.4	35.7	51.1	64.0
1989	13.3	21.7	36.9	51.8	64.7
1990	13.1	21.8	37.8	52.7	65.4
1992	16.0	24.4	40.3	53.4	65.5
1992	17.3	25.6	41.8	55.6	67.1
1993	17.6	26.9	43.8	58.0	69.2
1994	18.2	27.9	45.7	59.9	71.3
June 1995	17.6	27.1	45.3	60.0	71.5

Sources: NIC Database, Reports of Condition and Income; and Janet L. Yellen, Testimony before the Subcommittee on Financial Institutions and Consumer Credit, U.S. House of Representatives, October 17, 1995.

THE IMPACT OF INTERSTATE BANKING ON THE PUBLIC: COMPETITION AND DEPOSIT CONCENTRATION

As noted by Federal Reserve Board economist Dr. Stephen Rhoades (1985), interstate banking will undoubtedly lead (and, in some instances, has already led) to a significant increase in the concentration of banking industry resources at the national level. Yet this concentration trend need not happen necessarily at all levels in the economy, particularly at the local level for household and small business services in thousands of towns and cities across the United States. Moreover, evidence from an earlier study prepared by Rhoades (1983) suggests that credit allocation efficiency is not necessarily improved by the presence of larger, multiple-office banking organizations. This implies (as J. T. Rose and Donald Savage [1987] observe) that relatively small, locally oriented depository institutions can compete effectively against interstate banks on a *cost* basis.

However, there is evidence of substantial increases in nationwide banking concentration in recent years, as described in chapter 1. Note, for example, the trends depicted in table 5.8, which tracks the record from 1980 forward in the share of domestic bank assets held by the top five, top ten, top twenty-five, top fifty, and top one hundred U.S. banking organizations. These fig-

Table 5.9
Average Three-Firm Deposit Concentration Ratio for Metropolitan and Nonmetropolitan Areas, 1976–94 (FDIC-insured commercial banking organizations) (in percent)

Year	Metropolitan statistical areas (MSAs)	Non-metropolitan counties
1976	68.4	90.0
1977	67.8	89.9
1978	67.2	89.9
1979	66.7	89.7
1980	66.4	89.6
1981	66.0	89.4
1982	65.8	89.3
1983	65.9	89.4
1984	66.3	89.4
1985	66.7	89.4
1986	67.5	89.5
1987	67.7	89.5
1988	67.8	89.7
1989	67.5	89.7
1990	67.5	89.6
1991	66.7	89.3
1992	67.5	89.2
1993	66.8	89.2
1994	66.6	89.0

Sources: Summary of Deposits, 1976–1994; and Janet L. Yellen, Testimony before the Subcommittee on Financial Institutions and Consumer Credit, U.S. House of Representatives, October 17, 1995.

ures, compiled by Governor Janet Yellen (1995) of the Federal Reserve Board, show that whatever set of the largest U.S. banking companies looked at, this top group gained a significantly greater share of all domestic banking assets in the 1980s and early 1990s. The biggest jump in banking asset concentration seemed to center in the one hundred largest banking firms, which held about 51 percent of domestic assets in 1980 but rose to capture over 70 percent of all domestic banking assets by the summer of 1995. Even among the top twenty-five firms, domestic concentration rose from 33 percent in 1980 to 45 percent of all domestic banking assets in June 1995.

The banking concentration picture seems to change substantially, however, when the focus swings from a national to a *local*—metropolitan area and rural county—level. As the urban and rural figures in tables 5.9 and 5.10 seem to show, concentration in the American banking industry at the local level appears to have changed hardly at all, at least during the 1976–94 period reported in these figures supplied by the Federal Reserve Board. True, local banking markets average out to fairly high levels of concentration

Table 5.10
Average Herfindahl-Hirschmann Indexes (HHI) for Metropolitan Statistical Areas and Rural (Non-MSA) Counties, 1976–94

Year	Insured commercial banks only		Insured commercial banks plus 50% of savings banks and loan deposits	
	Metropolitan Statistical Areas (MSAs)	Non-MSA Counties	Metropolitan Statistical Areas (MSAs)	Non-MSA Counties
1976	1,951	4,504	N.A.	N.A.
1977	1,911	4,476	N.A.	N.A.
1978	1,884	4,451	N.A.	N.A.
1979	1,856	4,417	N.A.	N.A.
1980	1,843	4,396	N.A.	N.A.
1981	1,830	4,351	N.A.	N.A.
1982	1,845	4,340	N.A.	N.A.
1983	1,833	4,330	N.A.	N.A.
1984	1,848	4,341	1,356	3,782
1985	1,878	4,340	1,360	3,764
1986	1,911	4,325	1,388	3,744
1987	1,910	4,317	1,396	3,753
1988	1,912	4,292	1,400	3,726
1989	1,901	4,294	1,423	3,761
1990	1,906	4,266	1,458	3,788
1991	1,874	4,230	1,511	3,831
1992	1,906	4,189	1,563	3,832
1993	1,842	4,175	1,584	3,880
1994	1,825	4,142	1,602	3,873

Sources: Summary of Deposits data for banks and Survey of Savings data for thrifts. Pre-1985 HHIs calculated using 1985 MSA definitions; and Janet L. Yellen, Testimony before the Subcommittee on Financial Institutions and Consumer Credit, U.S. House of Representatives, October 17, 1995.

whether measured by the three-firm deposit concentration ratio (as in table 5.9) or by the Herfindahl-Hirschmann Index (HHI) (reported in table 5.10) which is the squared sum of all bank market shares in metropolitan and nonmetropolitan counties. On average across the United States, the three largest banking companies control two-thirds of the deposits in metropolitan statistical areas (MSAs) and nearly 90 percent of all deposits in smaller rural communities.

However, the "good" news is that these high concentration levels have scarcely moved at all since the mid-1970s. Moreover, because it is *local* markets where there is the most potential damage to consumers—particularly individuals, families, and small businesses—facing fewer service options and least able to find comparable services elsewhere, it is indeed "good news" that, thus far, concentration in local banking markets does not seem to be rising significantly. At the very least it is difficult to support the argument that banking concentration is increasing significantly in those local areas where the largest number of households and small businesses reside.

INTERSTATE EXPANSION AND ECONOMIES OF SCALE: ARE THERE COST BENEFITS FOR BANKS AND THE PUBLIC?

An extensive literature on the linkages between the size of a banking organization and its operating efficiency has emerged in the decades since World War II. (See, for example, Berger and Humphrey [1991], Clark [1988], Hunter and Timme [1991], Hunter, Timme, and Yang [1990], McAllister and McManus [1993], Noulas, Ray, and Miller [1990], and Bernstein [1996]). Despite numerous problems with data quality and statistical methodology these economies-of-scale studies point toward several pertinent conclusions:

1. Different banking services present different cost profiles, with some service-related costs highly size (volume) linked. Examples of high volume-sensitive bank services include checking accounts, savings accounts, and credit-card loans.

2. Economies of scale associated with individual bank offices (branches) are different and usually stronger than are scale economies measured across a whole banking organization, so that cost savings are more likely within the individual production unit rather than organization wide (with the possible exception of capital costs).

3. Economies across a whole banking organization appear to be modest at best. Once a banking firm reaches the moderate size range (usually $100 million to $500 million, or $1 billion in terms of total deposits or total assets), it appears to exhaust most of its potential for cost savings from continued growth in total output. Further increases in profitability must then come predominately from the revenue side of a banking firm.

4. More recently, there is at least some evidence that large, money-center banks do experience *some* cost economies, particularly with respect to capital costs, which appear to be appreciably lower for the largest banking organizations in the United States and abroad. If true, the lower average cost of capital experienced by larger banking firms grants them a significant production cost advantage (unless offset by greater

operating costs in other areas) over smaller banking companies.

Recent research studies (see especially Jayarante and Strahn [1995], Rhoades [1985], and Rose and Savage [1987]), then, find few cost savings from overall bank growth beyond $500 million to $1 billion in total assets or deposits. In general terms, research studies that include banks smaller than $1 billion in assets (such as Clark [1988], Berger and Humphrey [1991], and McAllister and McManus [1993]) find that average production unit costs generally begin to grow after a bank reaches $100 million to $500 million in aggregate assets, while research studies looking predominantly at the largest banks (with $1 billion or more in total assets, such as Hunter and Timme [1991] and Noulas, Ray, and Miller [1990]), find the lowest production costs in the $2 billion to $10 billion asset size range. However, growth beyond $10 billion in total assets seems to generate rising production costs (although McAllister and McManus [1993] find constant returns to scale once a bank climbs above $500 million in assets). In addition, a recent study by Bernstein (1996), which examines the impact of nonperforming loans on bank scale economies, finds that banks with high levels of troubled loans reach an optimum (lowest-cost) production level between $5 billion and $10 billion in total assets, but that a bank with substantially fewer (below-average) nonperforming loans can grow significantly larger before production costs begin to rise, perhaps as high as $50 billion in total assets. This latter result would seem to justify further consolidation of the banking system through interstate banking, but there are, as of yet, too few studies to confirm this research outcome.

Wherever the lowest-cost point is, once that least-cost production range is passed, a growing banking firm must look to *other factors* to enhance its net earnings over all costs, including its ability to enter new markets and new service lines that generate added revenues. On balance, it is not yet clear that interstate banking companies possess significant cost advantages over the more traditional intrastate banking firms. If interstate firms do possess significant economic advantages, they are more likely to lie on the revenue side of the banking ledger, residing in the superior capacity of larger banks, perhaps, to carry out both service and technological innovation, rather than on the cost side. Indeed, J. Akhavein, A. Berger, and D. Humphrey (1996) have recently found improvements in profit efficiency, rather than cost efficiency, when large banks merge, mainly due to a change in output mix from security investments to more loans.

Finally, research on organizational forms in the banking industry has identified a significant difference in operating costs between centralized and decentralized banking firms. That is, how far an interstate bank can lower its cost per unit of service produced and delivered may depend on whether its decision-making and operations functions are centralized in one or a few locations or widely dispersed so that local managers and staff play a more significant role in what is decided and how services are priced and delivered. Presumably in the long run, that bank organizational form that results in the lowest production and delivery costs will gradually come to dominate the industry.

As Federal Reserve Bank of Chicago economist Dr. William C. Hunter (1995) observes, research on organizational forms in banking and other industries has tended to focus on two extreme types of internal organization. With the so-called U form of organization, a bank would be divided into specialized departments, each performing an important function or functions, but decision-making is concentrated in top management. While the U form may promote cost savings through economies of scale, it can also have difficulty in trying to maximize profits due to several serious issues that often emerge. Hunter refers to these problem areas as bounded rationality (in which management is literally overwhelmed with information), opportunism (similar to agency problems in which some employees work to benefit themselves rather than the firm's stockholders), and subgoal targeting (such as attempting to maximize short-range objectives instead of working to achieve long-run maximization of the firm's value).

The contrasting organizational form is called M form. The M-form company is usually divided into semiautonomous operating units centered around particular services, territories, or markets. Strategic decisions that affect the long-run performance, service menus, facilities, and markets that the M-form firm will serve tend to be made by top management at the home office, but daily operating decisions are usually made by the firm's semiautonomous departments, which operate more like independent businesses—that is, as profit centers—than as merely departments within a larger organization.

What does recent research have to say about the relative desirability of U-form versus M-form banking organizations from a cost and performance point of view? Unfortunately, prior research has tended to focus on industries other than banking—that is, until Hunter (1995) published his study of 145 of the largest U.S. bank holding companies covering the October 1990 to July 1991 period. Complete data was received from 118 of the 145 bank CEOs interviewed by Hunter. These bank executives were asked questions about their company's internal organization, as reflected in the centralization or decentralization of credit administration, service pricing and delivery, back-office accounting, advertising, and computer facilities, and whether these banks were organized around functional areas or around customer or market groups.

Hunter found that all the banks interviewed contained some elements of an M-form-type organization. However, about half the sampled banks practiced centralized administration of the loan portfolio and service pricing decisions, while centralized product and service delivery systems prevailed in just over 60 percent of the sample banks. Moreover, the bulk of back-office processing and record-keeping functions (about 6 percent of the banks surveyed) were centralized in one or a few locations.

Hunter supplemented the survey information with financial statements for each bank in the sample extracted from the COMPUSTAT tapes. Using the dollar volume of deposits, business, consumer, and real estate loans, and noninterest income as measures of bank output, he found that a move toward more centralized decision making tended to *increase* bank operating costs. The estimated cost increase varied depending upon whether both bank operations and delivery systems were centralized. For example, if a bank whose delivery systems and operations were centralized moved toward centralized decision making as well, its operating costs seemed to rise nearly 4 percent, reducing its return on assets by about twenty-one basis points. On the other hand, a bank with decentralized delivery systems and centralized operations that moved toward greater centralization of decision making found its costs rising by nearly 10 percent, leading to a fifty-five basis point reduction in asset returns, on average. In *no* instance were operating costs lowered by greater centralization of bank management decision making.

For banks practicing centralized management decision making and operations, the movement towards a more centralized service delivery system appeared to have an insignificant effect on operating costs. However, if a banking company is already decentralized in its operations and decision functions, centralizing the service delivery mechanism tended to boost operating costs by about 6.5 percent, on average. The one centralization move that seemed to actually lower operating costs was the remaking of a bank's back-office operations toward greater centralization. Hunter estimated that completely decentralized banks (where service delivery, management decision making, and back-office functions are dispersed throughout the organization) display scale economies coefficient of 0.945, indicating that a 100 percent increase in output would result in a 94.5 increase in operating expenses, suggesting the presence of increasing returns to scale for this type of banking organization.

Overall, Hunter observed that *centralization* of bank decision-making functions is *not* an effective cost saver, but instead tends to add new costs. Centralization of service delivery mechanisms may result in no significant cost effect or operating costs may rise, but there is no indication that costs typically fall if service deliveries are centralized. However, centralization in back-office accounting, auditing, and computer functions *does* appear to save money with evidence of substantial economies of scale present in this functional area.

The results of this Chicago Federal Reserve Bank study are most interesting with substantial practical value for bank managements and stockholders if the study's results continue to stand up as further research takes place. Quite appropriately, the author stresses the need for caution in fully accepting his findings until further research can be done, refining the classification system for defining bank organizational types and examining a broader time period to make sure the results persist under a variety of market conditions. Nevertheless, the unfolding of research on bank organizational types needs to be encouraged and pressed forward if American banks are to remain competitive with other banks around the world.

THE IMPACT OF INTERSTATE BANKING ON CUSTOMER SERVICE AVAILABILITY, CONVENIENCE, AND PRICING

If interstate banking appears to score mixed results in terms of returns, risks, and costs, does it still make a positive contribution to greater service availability, greater convenience for the customer, and lower prices? Again, the verdict of recent research is decidedly mixed, indicating that the jury is still out regarding this important dimension of bank behavior and performance.

Serving Small Businesses

One of the greatest concerns today as interstate banking spreads across the nation is the fate of small businesses. In theory, at least, larger banks are able to make more loans of all types and are able to accept the greater risks associated with lending to smaller companies and new businesses. Moreover, larger banks can shift funds from market areas with excess deposits to those markets that have greater loan demand than their deposits will support. However, while small- and moderate-size banks often consider small, locally owned businesses as one of their key customer groups, many large banks seem to prefer to deal with larger corporate and institutional customers.

Texas is an apt illustration of the commonly held opinion that interstate banking and interstate branching could be harmful to the availability of loans for smaller business firms. Apparently the Texas legislature was convinced by those who argued that consolidation of the banking structure via interstate banking and branching would damage smaller firms and the development of local communities. Texas was the first major state to "opt out" of interstate branching. Certainly banks are critically important sources of credit for smaller business firms. For example, the National Survey of Small Business Finances (as reported on by Cole and Wolken [1995]) found that in 1995, the commercial banking sector was the single most important source of credit for small businesses.

Federal Reserve Bank of New York economists Philip Strahan and James Weston (1996) point out that, unlike publicly traded corporations, which generally have ready access to the open market in order to raise new capital, small businesses have more limited options and generally borrow at those lending institutions where long-term lender-borrower relationships have been established, reducing information costs and lowering the cost of credit for small enterprises. The smallest banks in the industry tend to grant more of these small relationship-type loans than do the largest of the industry's banks, which tend to focus on more objective standards in lending (including credit ratings, cash-flow projections, and financial ratio analysis). Small business loans are especially attractive to the smallest banks because fewer supporting services (such as cash management, risk hedging, and trust services) must be offered, which require expensive equipment and training. Moreover, smaller banks are more efficient at monitoring smaller loans than large banks are.

Then too, small banks face tight regulatory loan caps that place a maximum on the largest size loan they can create (which, by regulation, is tied to the size of the bank's capital and surplus account). Thus, smaller banks find small business loans attractive due to their limited size and because these loans help to promote diversification of their loan portfolio in order to reduce risk exposure.

Strahan and Weston (1996) point out that larger banks may *not necessarily* reduce their small business loans as the banks grow provided these loans are expected to be profitable. Indeed, they find that bank mergers typically do *not* reduce the share of bank loan portfolios devoted to small business credits and, in some cases, mergers appear to lead to increased commitments to small business lending, even in those instances where a large bank acquires a relatively small bank. Strahan and Weston examined 180 bank mergers taking place between June 1993 and June 1994, examining the proportion of small business loans relative to total assets made just before these mergers occurred and after the mergers were completed relative to a control group of banks not involved in merger activity. On average, the small business loan-to-asset ratio of the merging institutions rose from 8.3 to 8.5 percent over the study period, while banks not merger-involved experienced a decline in their small business loan ratios. Broken down by size group, small bank mergers appeared to result in increased small business lending, while larger banks showed essentially "no change" following their mergers. Moreover, as small banks are acquired by larger banking companies, these targeted small banks may be encouraged by their new owners to remain committed to the small business sector where they appear to have a comparative economic advantage in information costs.

Recently the federal banking agencies have been collecting data on small business loans (under $1 million each) from the Reports of Condition furnished by all U.S. federally supervised banks. Analysis of this condition report data reveals that large banks (over $1 billion in total assets) make just over half of all small business loans, while banks under $300 million in assets grant just over a third of all small business credits. These smallest institutions devote 8 to 9 percent of their total assets to small business loans (which represent well over 90 percent of their aggregate loans to the business sector), compared to less than 5 percent for banks over $1 billion in total assets (who commit less than 20 percent of their business credits to the smallest business borrowers).

Moreover, Strahan and Weston (1996) find that banks under $1 billion in assets that are affiliated with large bank holding companies (holding assets greater than $1 billion) make fewer small business loans than do independent banks and banks owned by small bank holding companies. However, they also find that banks with over $1 billion in assets hold more small business credits when they are controlled by the largest bank holding companies. Furthermore, these researchers found that the proportion of small business loans relative to total assets held by banks belonging to out-of-state holding companies was *not* significantly different from the proportion of small business loans held by banks controlled by holding companies based in the same state. Thus, the bank owners' *location* appears to have an insignificant impact on the portfolio commitment made by a bank to the small business sector. This finding is reinforced by Whalen (1995), who uncovers *no* adverse effects on the small business sector from acquisitions of banks in Illinois, Kentucky, and Montana by out-of-state banking companies.

Not everyone agrees with these findings, however. For example, Allen Berger, Anil Kashyap, and Joseph Scalise (1995) did a simulation study and found evidence that consolidation in the banking industry reduces credit flows toward smaller firms. Moreover, William Keeton (1995) observed that multiple-office bank firms tend to record smaller proportions of small business credits than do banking firms operating out of a single office.

A more recent study by economist Keeton (1996) finds that recent bank mergers, at least those in the Midwestern states served by the Kansas City Federal Reserve Bank, have tended to reduce local lending to businesses and farms. Many of the banks acquired became "junior partners" within larger bank holding companies. Perhaps as a result, business lending tended to decline when out-of-state banking firms bought out the previous owners of local banks. Yet, other, predominantly intrastate mergers that occurred did not appear, on average, to reduce local lending to area businesses, farms, and ranches. Dr. Keene hastened to add, however, that merely looking at the balance sheets of banks acquired by out-of-state companies may give a misleading picture because local loans may be originated at one bank and then transferred to another bank within the same company. Moreover, competing banks may step up their lending in response to a merger involving local firms. In this instance the *total* supply of credit to local businesses might not be reduced. Then, too, if out-of-state companies move loanable funds away from some local markets toward markets where expected returns were higher, this would tend to benefit the whole economy, which tends to work most efficiently when borrowed funds flow to their most productive employments.

A study by Levonian and Soller (1995) suggests that U.S. banks with assets of under $1 billion hold nearly *half* of all small business loans. Banks in the $50 million- to $100 million-size range appear to have the greatest proportion of small business loans relative to the size of their whole portfolio, but billion-dollar banks hold a much larger dollar total of small business credits. There is fear in the small business community that, if local banks are swallowed up by interstate companies, loanable funds in the banking sector will be redirected towards large corporations and governments and small businesses will come to claim a declining share of bank loan portfolios. Indeed, a recent study by Federal Reserve economists Joe Peek and Eric Rosengren (1995) found small business lending declining at some New England banks after these institutions were involved in an acquisition. Moreover, Allen Berger and Gregory Udell (1995), in a study of over nine hundred thousand bank loans, found that larger banks do tend to issue fewer loans to small business borrowers; however, they also tend to charge lower average loan rates (by about one hundred basis points) and require collateral less often (about 25 percent less of the time).

There is scattered evidence, then, that in some areas of the nation, larger banking companies put less emphasis on small business lending. However, there is, as of yet, no convincing evidence of a national trend in this direction. Besides, other lending institutions, such as credit unions, finance companies, and venture capital companies, appear to be moving to absorb some of the slack created by the withdrawal of more traditional small business lenders. Then, too, further consolidation of the banking industry could improve the stability of credit flowing to all businesses, large and small, because larger banks that have spread into different cities and towns and across state lines are no longer dependent on just a handful of local economies.

There is also an effort underway to develop a resale market for small business loans, which, if successful, could expand the number of lenders interested in this important corner of the credit marketplace. Indeed, banking structure specialist and business professor Dr. J. T. Rose (1986) concludes that interstate expansion should not be expected to adversely impact the cost or availability of credit to small businesses. Rose believes that cross-border banking may even enhance the development of the small business loan market, especially if interstate acquirers eventually turn to focus more and more of their acquisitions on small- and medium-size banks and work to increase the loan-asset ratios of these smaller banking firms.

INTERSTATE BANKING AND THE PRICES OF FINANCIAL SERVICES

The debate over the impact of multiple-office banking on market power and, therefore, on the public's access to competitively and efficiently priced financial services has been a long and contentious one. For example, opponents of the geographic spread of branch banking have generally argued that allowing banks to expand across the countryside via merger and acquisition has enhanced the market power of these institutions at public expense, allowing banks with multiple offices to reap excess returns through less-than-competitive pricing practices and, on occasion, though explicit or implicit collusion. It is alleged that multiple-branch banking firms routinely charge higher prices for their services, both because of greater market power and due to greater operating costs.

Proponents of bank branch office expansion, on the other hand, contend that allowing banking firms to expand geographically without constraints on their organizational form tends to stimulate competition. This happens allegedly because bank geographic expansion lowers entry barriers into what were previously sheltered markets. Thus, bank customers will receive more services, though not necessarily lower prices.

The evidence for or against these opposing arguments is mixed, though more recent studies have tended to be more supportive of increasing branch banking's territorial powers. For example, a relatively new study by Paul Calem and Leonard Nakamura (1995) suggests that bank branching tends to offset any localized market power that may exist by expanding the geographic scope of competition. Services offered through so-called peripheral locations appear to be priced more competitively and more uniformly when these locations are reached by bank branch networks. These authors develop a theoretical model that suggests that bank branching engenders more uniform pricing across different locations than would be true if outlying areas were served only by independent banks, which tend to price their services in such a way as to capture the surplus of locally limited consumers. In effect, branch banking tends to export competition from dense metropolitan markets toward outlying market areas.

These arguments were tested by Calem and Nakamura (1995), employing deposit interest rate survey data for pairs of banks drawn from limited branching states. These two Federal Reserve Board economists found substantially larger price differentials for pairs of banks drawn from states where branch banking is restricted. This outcome seems to hold even within the boundaries of a limited geographic area, such as the same or an adjacent metropolitan area or county. Thus, interest returns on deposits offered to the public appeared to be higher where branch banking was largely unrestricted, suggesting that savers benefit from purchasing thrift accounts in a branch banking environment.

INTERSTATE BANKING, ECONOMIC GROWTH, AND NEW JOBS

Finally, advocates of interstate banking have expressed the belief that the nation as a whole should benefit, not only because the banking system should be more stable, but because of efficiencies in resource allocation and greater competition. If the nation's scarce resources are more efficiently marshaled to pursue those investment projects with the highest expected rates of return and if competition among financial-service providers increases, then the country should grow faster and more new jobs will be generated as a result of expanding investments in plant and equipment.

Unfortunately, these claims for a faster growing and more prosperous economy are, today at least, merely unproven assertions. Not only is the experience with full-service interstate banking too recent to provide a foundation to support such claims, but also earlier research on banking structure calls the whole idea into question. As Jerome Darnell (1973) notes, research studies attempting to find links between a state's banking structure— whether or not a state is dominated by branch banks, unit (single-office) banks, or bank holding companies—and its economic growth and development generally find little, if any, relationship.

There appear to be fast-growing states (like Florida and Texas, for example) that previously restricted branch banking for many decades just as there are fast-growing states (like Arizona) that allow statewide branching and entry from any other state in the nation for bank holding companies. The structure of a state's or a region's banking industry appears to be of secondary importance when compared to its natural resources, access to navigable rivers and seaports, the presence or absence of physical barriers to transportation and communication, and scores of other factors directly related to the production and delivery of goods and services. No one has yet demonstrated that the trend toward interstate banking necessarily brings with it greater economic progress and an improved standard of living for the nation's population.

OVERVIEW OF THE RESEARCH LITERATURE

Overall, the research evidence generated thus far on the performance effects of interstate bank expansion appears to be in conflict and seems to lack findings of either consistent benefits or consistent costs for the individual firm and for the public resulting from the spread of interstate banking. This is a field that seems heavily laden with *unresolved issues*. Researchers do know that most of the gains from interstate expansion appear to flow to the stockholders of banks *acquired* by interstate banking companies, though in recent years there is at least some evidence that the shareholders of interstate acquiring banks do receive some slight excess returns as acquisitions are made across state lines. While interstate firms frequently advertise "cost cutting" and added revenues as motives for crossing state lines, it is not clear that either benefit accrues in a majority of cases. The jury is still out regarding the economic benefits of having an interstate banking system, at least as far as the owners of these organizations and the public are concerned. If there are real benefits to be had from interstate banking, researchers seemed to have found them mainly in greater public convenience and broader bank service menus, not necessarily in lower costs and greater efficiency in utilizing the nation's scarce resources.

NOTES

1. The rate of return on a bank's total assets equals the ratio of its net income after taxes and all other operating expenses divided by its total assets. Thus, asset returns measure the efficiency with which the management and staff of a bank can convert its total resources (assets) into net earnings.

2. Interest income and fees earned on loans represent the largest source of revenue for most banks, averaging close to 70 percent of total operating revenues across the U.S. banking industry in recent years. Loan-loss provision is an annual noncash operating expense that appears on a bank's income statement. As banks come to expect greater loan losses, the provision for loan losses is increased and added to the bank's bad-debt reserve, which appears on the balance sheet and is usually referred to as the allowance for loan losses.

CHAPTER 6

How Bankers Evaluate Target Interstate Markets and Institutions Across State Lines

What factors do bankers weigh when they decide to cross state lines and make an acquisition? What features of a state or local area seem to draw the most attention from interstate acquirers? What makes an individual bank attractive as an interstate acquisition target?

Evidence on the factors bankers actually consider in entering new markets and in choosing a particular bank to acquire is sparse indeed. Bankers usually don't like to publish with any specificity the features of a target market or a target banking firm they value most highly for fear of giving away their company's strategic plan to competitors. If a particular formula for identifying and making acquisitions is working well, successful bankers obviously would prefer to keep that formula to themselves.

Moreover, as Edward W. Kelley, Jr. (1995), member of the Federal Reserve Board, noted recently in a speech to the American Institute of Certified Public Accountants, several different interstate expansion strategies have been followed by leading American banks, and many of these different, often conflicting strategies have been quite successful. For example, Chase Manhattan and Chemical Bank of New York have pursued consolidation largely within their existing market areas; First Union, First Fidelity, NBD Bancorp, and First Chicago Corporation have tried to link adjoining markets together; while NationsBank and Bank of America have ventured far afield in the Southwest, Southeast, Midwest, and the Middle Atlantic regions. Therefore, the track record of interstate banking, thus far, suggests there is *no one path to banking success* in today's marketplace.

However, what researchers *do* know of the interstate banking acquisition process by observing the pattern of recent acquisitions across state lines suggests that most interstate companies engage in a *two-step process*:

1. They evaluate and choose the region, state, and community they wish to enter, looking most closely at it's overall economic, financial, and demographic features.

2. Once a target market area or region is chosen, individual banks within that desired area are evaluated to identify the most desirable banking firms as possible acquisition candidates.

This chapter looks at the key marketwide (macro) and individual (micro) features bankers appear to consider when they acquire banking firms in other states.

THE MACRO OR MARKET VIEW: ECONOMIC, FINANCIAL, AND DEMOGRAPHIC FEATURES OF NEWLY ENTERED BANKING MARKETS

The Search for Core Deposits

One of the dominant factors in many interstate banking strategies today is access to *new deposits*. Bankers like to enter and build a base for future expansion in those states that generate the heaviest deposit volumes. Interstate expansion is often a vehicle for attracting the most loyal "core deposits," which are expected to stay with a bank even through wide swings in interest rates and economic conditions. The accepted definition of "core deposits" focuses on the *interest-rate elasticity* of these funds—core deposits have very limited sensitivity to interest-rate movements, so they remain loyal to a bank even through substantial changes in the overall level of market interest rates. Most core deposits arise from household and small business customers and generally involve deposits well under $100,000 apiece, unlike volatile money-market accounts ("hot money"), which flow into and out of a bank on short notice as market interest rates change. State and local areas that seem to promise strong growth in these more stable deposit sources usually appear high on most interstate bank acquisition lists.

As table 6.1 relates, states that top the list in the volume of available deposits held include New York, California, Illinois, Texas, Pennsylvania, Florida, Ohio, Michigan, New Jersey, Maryland, Georgia, North Carolina, Missouri, Virginia, and Connecticut. It shouldn't be a surprise to learn that

Table 6.1

U.S. States with the Greatest Volume of Total Deposits, Loans, and Equity Capital

State	Deposit Volume and Rank		Loan Volume and Rank		Capital Volume and Rank	
	Deposit Rank	Total Deposits (in billions)	Loan Rank	Total Loans (in billions)	Capital Rank	Equity Capital (in billions)
New York	1	$560.1	1	$556.5	1	$62.3
California	2	268.9	2	223.2	2	27.3
Illinois	3	164.3	3	117.7	3	18.4
Texas	4	152.6	7	99.3	5	14.7
Pennsylvania	5	136.4	4	117.7	4	16.1
Florida	6	135.1	5	103.8	6	12.7
Ohio	7	106.2	6	100.0	7	10.8
Michigan	8	82.8	8	70.3	10	7.8
New Jersey	9	80.7	12	53.5	9	8.2
Maryland	10	68.0	11	56.2	11	7.6
Georgia	11	66.9	9	66.4	8	8.9
North Carolina	12	66.8	10	61.4	12	6.7
Missouri	13	58.4	14	41.8	13	5.7
Virginia	14	57.3	13	45.0	14	5.5
Connecticut	15	50.9	15	41.7	15	5.4

Note:
As of March 31, 1995.

Source: Board of Governors of the Reserve System.

these states are among the leading areas for interstate acquisitions and also include those states where the majority of the largest interstate bank holding companies are currently based.

Refining the deposit measure a bit, the ratio of a state's small deposits (under $100,000) to the total of all its banking assets can be calculated. Such a ratio would yield a rough measure of the amount of core deposits—the most stable deposit base a bank can access—held by banks in each state. Deposit figures provided by the Federal Deposit Insurance Corporation for 1994 show that the state with the highest portion of core deposits is Colorado (with an 80.6 percent ratio of total deposits less time deposits over $100,000 in denomination relative to total banking assets in the state). Other leading states with exceptionally high ratios of core deposits (excluding time deposits over $100,000) to total banking assets include Arkansas (75.7 percent), California (74.2 percent), Indiana (72.5 percent), Iowa (76.0 percent), Kansas (76.8 percent), Louisiana (74.8 percent), Maryland (74.4 percent), Missouri (76.0 percent), Montana (80.3 percent), Nebraska

(78.3 percent), New Jersey (76.9 percent), North Dakota (79.6 percent), Texas (73.2 percent), Virginia (71.0 percent), Washington (73.1 percent), and Wisconsin (73.7 percent). The foregoing list includes several states— California, Indiana, Iowa, Maryland, New Jersey, Texas, Virginia, and Washington—that have been among the leading areas of the nation in the volume and intensity of interstate banking activity.

The Search for New Loan Demand

The search for profitable new loan relationships also appears to be a major motivating factor driving interstate bank expansion. States in which loan bookings are high represent attractive target areas because loan growth translates into revenue growth in the form of interest on outstanding loans plus fee income from loan-related fee-generating services (such as fees charged for loan commitments and the servicing of loans). Among the leading states in total loans booked (as table 6.1 reveals) are New York, California, Illinois, Pennsylvania, Florida, Ohio, and Texas—all states that have attracted large-scale interstate acquisition activity.

To most interstate banking companies today, *loans* are the foundation stone of a profitable bank-customer relationship. Generally, customers' deposits follow their loans, so that a bank willing to grant more loans gains both loan revenues and a growing deposit base from which to grant new loans in the future. When a bank holds *both* a customer's loan and deposit accounts, other service requests normally follow quickly, such as the customer's need to wire funds or purchase safekeeping space in the bank's vault. In the language of modern banking, loans serve as the initial service base upon which to build "relationship banking." Once a customer has purchased at least three or four services from a bank, there is greater customer dependence on that institution and the customer usually finds it significantly more difficult to transfer his or her account to another bank. In effect, the customer becomes increasingly tied to a particular banking firm and less inclined to search for a banking relationship with another institution.

The Search for Additional Capital

Beginning in the late 1980s and particularly after the adoption of the Basle Agreement in 1988 and passage of the FDIC Improvement Act of 1991 in the United States, the pressure on banks and bank holding companies to achieve and maintain strong capital positions became intense. The Basle Agreement, signed by the United States, Japan, Canada, and the nations of Western Europe, required all banks headquartered in these countries to hold a minimum amount of capital equal to no less than 8 percent of their total risk-adjusted assets. Moreover, owners' equity—the most stable long-term funding base for a bank—must support no less than 4 percent of a bank's total risk-weighted assets.

The dictates of the Basle Agreement were further strengthened in 1991 when the U.S. Congress passed the FDIC Improvement Act. This stringent law made bank capital the centerpiece of regulation for the American banking system, tying the size of a U.S. bank's capital (relative to its risk-exposed assets) to the degree to which it could expect to be placed under regulatory pressure. Banks with capital ratios above the minimums required by law could expect to receive little regulatory resistance to their plans for acquisitions and mergers and the offering of new services. Banks whose capital-to-risk-assets ratio dropped below the legal minimum would, on the other hand, be confronted with substantial regulatory roadblocks until their capital was strengthened.

For example, U.S. banks whose capital-to-risk-assets ratio was 10 percent or higher could expect to have their expansion plans approved, provided there were no violations of federal or state law involved. Banks whose capital ratio was below 10 percent but at least 8 percent would also find few regulatory barriers to their expansion but would be prohibited from paying stockholder dividends high enough to erode their capital position and result in a capital-to-risk asset ratio of less than 8 percent. Those federally supervised U.S. banks with capital ratios below 8 percent must expect to encounter, not only increased resistance to their plans for expansion, but also increased government involvement in several basic management decisions, such as whether to award employees pay raises or bonuses. If a bank's ratio of tangible equity capital to assets drops below 2 percent, that institution is potentially subject to seizure and sale by the Federal Deposit Insurance Corporation. Clearly, this stringent law applies great pressure to U.S. banking organizations seeking to expand, placing capital adequacy as a factor to reckon with in their strategic plans for tapping interstate markets.

Hundreds of U.S. banks and banking companies have recently sold stock and debentures to increase their holdings of long-term capital and increase their ratios of total capital to risk-exposed assets. However, sale of stock is an expensive source of bank capital, and the generation of internal capital through retained earnings can be a slow capital-building process. An important alternative to selling new equity shares or generating higher retained earnings is to merge with banks and bank holding companies already displaying strong capital positions. States and regions where the supply of long-term bank capital is relatively large, therefore, represent attractive acquisition targets. As table 6.1 shows, these areas include New York, California, Illinois, Pennsylvania, Texas, Florida, Ohio, and Georgia.

Projected Growth in Population

Interstate banks have tended to flow toward those areas evidencing strong population growth, stressing that more rapid increases in an area's underlying population generates not only new deposits but also future loan demand and revenues from the sale of both traditional and innovative new

Table 6.2
Population Projections for U.S. States Showing Their Projected Total
Population Ranks in 2020

Projected Fastest Growing Group of States in Total Population	Projected State Rank in the year 2020	Projected Moderate Growing States in Total Population	Projected State Rank in the Year 2020	Projected Slowest Growing Group of States in Total Population	Projected State Rank in the Year 2020
Alaska	46	Alabama	22	Connecticut	29
Arizona	20	Arkansas	33	Illinois	5
California	1	Delaware	45	Iowa	32
Colorado	24	Kansas	30	Indiana	14
Florida	3	Louisiana	23	Kentucky	27
Georgia	9	Maryland	17	Maine	41
Hawaii	39	Minnesota	21	Massachusetts	16
Idaho	40	Missouri	18	Michigan	8
Nevada	36	New Hampshire	42	Mississippi	31
New Mexico	35	Nebraska	37	New York	4
Oregon	26	New Jersey	10	North Dakota	48
Texas	2	North Carolina	11	Ohio	7
Utah	34	Oklahoma	28	Pennsylvania	6
Washington	13	South Carolina	25	Rhode Island	43
Washington, D.C.	51	South Dakota	47	Vermont	50
Wyoming	49	Tennessee	15	West Virginia	38
		Virginia	12		
		Wisconsin	19		

Sources: U.S. Bureau of the Census; and Federal Reserve Bank of Minneapolis, *Fedgazette,* VI,
No. 3 (July 1994), p. 28.

banking services. In 1993 the U.S. Bureau of the Census developed population projections for the fifty states, estimating the percentage change in
total population from 1993 to 2020 based upon recent demographic
changes and other factors. The states were divided into three groups based
on their projected rate of change in population over the 1993–2020 period:
(a) 1.0 to 15.0, (b) 15.1 to 30.0, and (c) 30.0 to 55.5 percentage point
changes in population. The key states that fit into each of these groups are
shown in table 6.2.

There is little question that interstate companies have been highly sensitive
to the projected population growth of selected states and regions. Interstate
acquisitions accelerated during the 1980s and early 1990s into such states
as Arizona, California, Colorado, Georgia, Florida, Texas, Utah, and Wash-

Table 6.3
Interstate BHC Acquisitions of Banks by Region, 1980–95
(Numbers of banks acquired, by state)

West		Midwest		Southeast	
Alaska	4	Iowa	14	Alabama	11
Arizona	24	Illinois	140	Arkansas	3
California	3	Indiana	29	Delaware	10
Colorado	67	Kansas	34	Florida	58
Idaho	3	Kentucky	3	Georgia	22
Montana	4	Michigan	6	Louisiana	3
New Mexico	38	Minnesota	23	Maryland	15
Nevada	5	Missouri	4	North Carolina	5
Oregon	9	North Dakota	3	South Carolina	7
Utah	8	Nebraska	25	Tennessee	43
Washington	16	Ohio	7	Virginia	10
Wyoming	35	South Dakota	1	West Virginia	25
		Wisconsin	10		
Totals	216	Totals	299	Totals	212

Southwest		New England		Middle Atlantic	
Oklahoma	32	Connecticut	9	New Jersey	13
Texas	176	Massachusetts	9	New York	12
New Mexico	38	Maine	13	Pennsylvania	10
		New Hampshire	5		
		Rhode Island	1		
		Vermont	1		
Totals	246	Totals	38	Totals	35

Source: Data files assembled by the author from individual bank and bank holding company acquisition decisions by the Federal Reserve Board as reported in the weekly H.2 data release.

ington, which have been among the nation's leaders in actual population growth over the past decade and whose projected population growth currently lies among the top third of all states.

These projected population growth figures match up rather well with the actual interstate acquisitions undertaken by the U.S. banking industry since 1980. The author has been compiling a comprehensive list of all bank acquisitions from 1980 forward from the Federal Reserve Board's weekly H-2 release of merger and acquisitions. As table 6.3 shows, the greatest number of interstate acquisitions over the 1980–95 period were congregated largely in the Southeast, West, Southwest, and Midwest regions, where some of the most rapidly growing states in terms of population are situated. More-

Table 6.4
Acquisitions of Banks in Leading Cities by Interstate Banking Companies, 1980–95 (Numbers of banks acquired, by city)

West		Southwest	
Phoenix-Scottsdale, AZ	22	Oklahoma City, OK	18
Denver, CO	11	Austin, TX	6
Salt Lake City, UT	6	Dallas, TX	22
Cheyenne, WY	5	Houston, TX	41
Albuquerque, NM	15	El Paso, TX	9
		San Antonio, TX	6
Southeast		**Midwest**	
Bradenton, FL	17	Chicago, IL	5
Baltimore, MD	5	Springfield, IL	7
		Indianapolis, IN	4
		Peoria, IL	8
		Lincoln, NE	4
New England		Omaha, NE	6
Boston, MA	5		
Portland, ME	4		

Source: Data files assembled by the author from individual bank and bank holding company acquisition decisions by the Federal Reserve Board as reported in the weekly H.2 data release.

over, the leading cities in these regions have attracted a disproportionate share of all cross-border bank acquisitions, as reflected by the data presented in table 6.4. Among the more important cities recently targeted for interstate bank acquisitions have been Dallas and Houston, Texas; Oklahoma City, Oklahoma; Chicago and Springfield, Illinois; Boston, Massachusetts; Phoenix-Scottsdale, Arizona; Denver, Colorado; Baltimore, Maryland; and Albuquerque, New Mexico.

Note, however, that the figures in tables 6.3 and 6.4 reflect the number of separate banking companies acquired and not the dollar volume of banking assets involved in these acquisitions. By counting the number of firms acquired, the tendency exists to give extra weight to the smallest banks, so that cities, states, and regions where small banks dominate (as in the Southwest and Midwest) assume greater relative importance. In terms of dollars of assets changing hands in cross-border acquisitions, the states of California, Florida, Illinois, New York, New Jersey, Ohio, Pennsylvania, Texas, and Massachusetts have occupied leading positions within the interstate movement.

Table 6.5
Bank Performance by Region, First Quarter of 1996

U. S. Regions	Annual Growth in Net Income	Return on Assets (ROA)	Return on Equity Capital (ROE)	Net Interest Margin (NIM)	Net Loans Charged-Off to Loans and Leases	Annual Growth in Total Bank Assets
Northeast	20.3	1.01	11.20	3.47	.027	4.9

(Connecticut, Washington, D. C., Maine, Maryland, Massachusetts, New Hampshire, New Jersey, New York, Pennsylvania, Puerto Rico, Rhode Island, Vermont, U.S. Virgin Islands)

Southeast	-8.2	0.88	9.31	3.41	0.33	-15.6

(Alabama, Florida, Georgia, Mississippi, North Carolina, South Carolina, Tennessee, Virginia, West Virginia)

North Central	15.4	0.92	10.06	3.06	0.11	2.6

(Illinois, Indiana, Kentucky, Michigan, Ohio, Wisconsin)

Midwest	-11.4	0.90	10.59	3.02	0.12	-4.6

(Iowa, Kansas, Minnesota, Missouri, Nebraska, North Dakota, South Dakota)

Southwest	266.7	2.62	34.12	2.98	0.24	10.0

(Arkansas, Louisiana, New Mexico, Oklahoma, Texas)

West	120.0	0.69	9.5	2.99	0.46	-3.1

(Alaska, Arizona, California, Colorado, Hawaii, Idaho, Montana, Nevada, Oregon, Pacific Islands, Utah, Washington, and Wyoming)

Notes:

Net income is measured by total operating revenues less all operating expenses (including taxes) plus any extraordinary gains (or minus any extraordinary losses) net of taxes. Return on assets and equity capital equal net after-tax income divided by total assets or total equity capital, respectively. The net interest margin equals all interest revenues less interest expenses, while net loans charged off represent loans declared worthless by the banks holding them less any recoveries on previously charged-off loans.

Source: Federal Deposit Insurance Corporation, *The FDIC Quarterly Banking Profile,* Washington, D.C., 1st quarter 1996.

U.S. States and Regions Experiencing Above-Average Bank Profitability and Growth

States and regions where banks are experiencing above-average profitability and growth also tend to attract the most attention from interstate companies. As shown in table 6.5, banks in the Southwest, Northeast, and North Central states, have recently led the nation in rates of return on total bank assets (ROA). The Southwest has led other regions in terms of return on equity (ROE), followed by the Northeast and Midwest.

Bankers in the 1980s and early 1990s also became highly sensitized to loan portfolio quality as their net charge-offs of bad loans (that is, total charge-offs of worthless loans less any recoveries from previously charged-off loans) soared. In 1996, for example, as table 6.5 indicates, the West, Southeast, and Northeast led all other regions in net loan loss charge-offs relative to their total loans. However, the North Central, Midwest, and Southwestern regions reported the lowest loan-loss ratios by the mid-1990s, helping to explain the recent attractiveness of these regions for interstate bank entry. In terms of growth in bank income and assets, the Southwest ranked number one in 1996, followed by the Western and Northeastern regions of the country, where interstate acquisitions were taking place in record numbers.

An Adequate Supply of Banks and Bank Offices Available as Acquisition Targets

States and regions with a relatively high proportion of banks and banking offices available for acquisition have also proven to be attractive acquisition targets because interstate banking firms have generally preferred to acquire existing banks and bank offices rather than starting new (*de novo*) facilities. As table 6.6 indicates, the state of Illinois leads the list with more depository institutions—including commercial banks, savings banks, and savings and loans—as potential acquisition targets than any other state, followed closely by Texas, Minnesota, California, Florida, Georgia, Ohio, and Pennsylvania. All of these states have been focal points for extensive interstate merger and acquisition activity in recent years.

States containing sizable numbers of branch offices have also ranked high on the interstate acquisitions list for those banking organizations interested in acquiring ready-made service distribution systems. Among the most prominent states with extensive branching systems in place, as table 6.7 shows, are California, New York, Pennsylvania, and Florida—four states where interstate acquisitions have become a significantly important tool for transforming banking into a consolidated service industry.

While bank branch office systems have been much maligned in recent years due to their high operating cost, bankers with large branch systems have found that locational convenience still matters to most of their household and small business customers. With the possible exception of insurance agencies and finance companies, few nonbank financial-service firms have established elaborate branching systems, which gives bankers a competitive advantage over many of their nonbank competitors offering the same or similar services. Moreover, bankers have found ways to reduce branching's costs through such devices in-store facilities (e.g., offices inside grocery stores, retail shops, and shopping malls) and automated deposit and credit

Table 6.6
States with the Largest Number of Insured Depository Institutions as Potential Acquisition Targets

States	BIF Members*	SAIF Members*	Total Insured Depository Institutions
Illinois	907	160	1,067
Texas	980	60	1,040
Minnesota	560	25	585
Iowa	516	34	550
Missouri	471	58	529
California	399	92	491
Kansas	455	27	482
Wisconsin	400	53	453
Florida	348	88	436
Ohio	255	170	425
Georgia	378	45	423
Pennsylvania	250	125	375
Nebraska	349	18	367
Oklahoma	350	12	362
Kentucky	285	54	339
Indiana	223	81	304
Colorado	279	16	295
New York	222	65	287

Notes:
As of December 31, 1994.
BIF institutions include all commercial banks and some savings banks whose deposits are insured by the Bank Insurance Fund of the Federal Deposit Insurance Corporation, while SAIF members are savings associations whose deposits are granted insurance coverage by the Savings Association Insurance Fund (also a division of the FDIC).

Source: Federal Deposit Insurance Corporation, *Statistics on Banking,* Washington, D.C., 1994.

machines that provide basic services with minimal cost in terms of bank personnel.

The Search for Less Competitive Markets

Some interstate organizations prefer less competitive markets that have adequate economic growth and permit them to collect higher service fees from their customers. Frequently, these markets are centered in small- and medium-size suburban communities surrounding such cities as Atlanta, Boston, Chicago, Dallas, Houston, Los Angeles, and Miami, served by no more than two or three locally based banks.

Banking researchers Edward Kane (1995), O. M. W. Sprague (1993), and Burton Abrams and Russell Settle (1993) have recently developed a rent-

Table 6.7
States with the Largest Number of Insured Banking Offices

States	Total Branch Offices	Unit Banking Institutions	Institutions Operating Branches	Total FDIC-Insured Institutions	All Banking Offices
California	6,747	107	384	491	7,238
New York	4,577	81	206	287	4,864
Pennsylvania	4,143	75	300	375	4,518
Florida	3,950	103	333	436	4,386
Ohio	3,603	132	293	425	4,028
Texas	2,936	531	509	1,040	3,976
Illinois	2,321	474	593	1,067	3,388
Michigan	2,790	29	202	231	3,021
New Jersey	2,751	36	148	184	2,935
North Carolina	2,425	32	110	142	2,567
Virginia	2,199	35	167	202	2,401
Indiana	1,899	66	238	304	2,203
Georgia	2,705	142	281	423	2,128
Massachusetts	1,669	72	194	265	1,934

Note:
As of December 31, 1994.

Source: Federal Deposit Insurance Corporation, *Statistics on Banking,* Washington, D.C. 1994.

seeking theory that argues that the older restrictions against branch banking and interstate banking (as reflected in the McFadden-Pepper and Glass-Steagall Acts discussed earlier in chapter 2) were set up to allow local banks to earn monopoly or quasi-monopoly rents from those customers (particularly households and small businesses) who have few banking alternatives. Anthony Cyrnak and Stephen Rhoades (1989), in a study of more than eleven thousand U.S. banks, found a strong *inverse relationship* between the number of banks in a market and average bank profitability, with the highest asset returns in markets served by only one, two, or three banks. These two researchers conclude that "small concentrated banking markets can offer banking organizations a potentially profitable avenue for expansion—and may present fewer risks to the acquiring firm" (1989, p. 26). New banks, including interstate banking organizations, hope to enter these special markets where monopoly or quasi-monopoly rents are present and compete any excess returns away. Less-competitive local markets also often contain sizable packets of core deposits that supply low-cost, long-term funding for the banks involved.

Negative or Low Positive Correlations with Current Bank Returns

Interstate banking firms could also benefit from entry into new areas where bank earnings are negatively correlated or display a low positive correlation with bank earnings from their established market areas. Geographic diversification of this sort would tend to reduce bank earnings and cash-flow risk. Unfortunately, as shown in chapter 5, there are apparently few states that generate negative or even low positive bank earnings correlations with other states. Table 6.8 shows that widely dispersed states sometimes do display low or negative intercorrelations of bank earnings (measured by ROA). Across all sizes of banks, such pairs of states as California and Maryland, California and Connecticut, Maine and Washington, and Delaware and New York display negative earnings correlations, suggesting risk-reducing potential for an interstate organization able to combine banks acquired from these particular states.

The discussion in chapter 5 suggests that the greatest potential for low earnings correlations appears to center among smaller banks (for example, those under $100 million in total assets). As table 6.8 indicates, attractive combinations for small banks include such pairs of states as California and South Carolina, Illinois and Pennsylvania, and Delaware and Virginia. The worst combinations (from a positive earnings correlation point of view) tend to center in the Midwest—for example, such two-state combinations as Arkansas and South Dakota and Connecticut and New Jersey—where recent bank earnings ratios display a 98 percent positive intercorrelation. If earnings diversification is an important goal, interstate banking companies would do well to reach outside their own narrow geographic regions into distant states and cities with attractive economic, financial, and demographic profiles.

A Warning Note on State and Local Taxation

Finally, in assessing target states and local areas, banks planning interstate ventures are increasingly being made aware of differences in tax exposure that may accompany different strategies for geographic expansion. Indeed, any gains in operating efficiency or savings in operating expenses could be substantially reduced by incurring heavy local tax burdens. The fifty states vary considerably in the rates they charge for franchise, income, property, or unemployment taxes. Examples include Indiana, Massachusetts, Pennsylvania, and West Virginia, which have above-average tax rates on bank income. Moreover, some states, such as Florida and Wisconsin, can tax out-of-state firms even though no office facility resides inside their territory. One of the reasons the Riegle-Neal Interstate Banking Act delayed permission for full-service interstate branching until 1997 was to give the individual

Table 6.8
Examples of the "Best" and the "Worst" Potential Interstate Banking Combinations of Pairs of States

The "Best" Two-State Combinations (Maximum Negative Correlations of ROA)							
All Banks		Large Banks		Medium Banks		Small Banks	
Hawaii/Vermont	-0.623	Maryland/Montana	-0.626	Connecticut/Wyoming	-0.830*	Hawaii/South Carolina	-0.904*
Maine/Wyoming	-0.605	Hawaii/Virginia	-0.582	Delaware/Vermont	-0.818*	Idaho/Tennessee	-0.890*
Vermont/Washington	-0.590			Idaho/New Jersey	-0.815*	Arkansas/Delaware	-0.885*
Connecticut/Wyoming	-0.583			Delaware/New York	-0.813*	Arkansas/Maryland	-0.881*
Oklahoma/Vermont	-0.579			Connecticut/Montana	-0.809*	Illinois/Pennsylvania	-0.873*
California/Maryland	-0.578			Connecticut/Oregon	-0.807*	Arkansas/South Carolina	-0.872*
D.C./Washington	-0.567			New York/Wyoming	-0.779*	California/South Carolina	-0.870*
California/Connecticut	-0.555			Connecticut/Michigan	-0.761*	Connecticut/Idaho	-0.864*
D.C./Oklahoma	-0.553			New York/Oregon	-0.779*	Delaware/Virginia	-0.862*
Maine/Montana	-0.550			California/Kentucky	-0.755*	Kansas/Vermont	-0.857*
Hawaii/New Jersey	-0.550					Arkansas/Indiana	-0.857*
Connecticut/Montana	-0.542					Alabama/Hawaii	-0.852*
Michigan/Vermont	-0.541					Arizona/South Carolina	-0.847*
Maine/Washington	-0.539					Indiana/Iowa	-0.852*
Montana/Vermont	-0.538					Alabama/Hawaii	-0.852*
Nebraska/Vermont	-0.536					Arizona/South Carolina	-0.847*
D.C./Montana	-0.535					Colorado/Pennsylvania	-0.840*
Hawaii/Virginia	-0.535					Hawaii/Indiana	-0.840*
						Iowa/South Carolina	-0.839*
						Delaware/Hawaii	-0.834*

The "Worst" Two-State Combinations (Statistically Significant Positive Correlations of ROA)							
All Banks		**Large Banks**		**Medium Banks**		**Small Banks**	
Arkansas/South Dakota	0.989*			Washington D.C./Vermont	0.960*	Kansas/West Virginia	0.939*
Connecticut/New Jersey	0.987*	Nebraska/Vermont	0.996*	Massachusetts/New Jersey	0.959*	Connecticut/Vermont	0.939*
Florida/New Hampshire	0.986*	Arizona/Arkansas	0.995*	Oklahoma/Oregon	0.958*	Arizona/Washington D. C.	0.924*
Idaho/Iowa	0.980*	Tennessee/Vermont	0.995*	Montana/Oregon	0.954*	Arkansas/Arizona	0.914*
Florida/Kentucky	0.979*	Arkansas/Wyoming	0.995*	Ohio/Wisconsin	0.953*	Arkansas/Virginia	0.909*
Florida/Tennessee	0.978*	Mississippi/New Hampshire	0.994*	Louisiana/Oregon	0.953*	Washington D. C./Iowa	0.909*
Idaho/South Dakota	0.972*	Louisiana/West Virginia	0.993*	Maryland/South Dakota	0.953*	Arkansas/Washington D. C.	0.901*
Kansas/Michigan	0.971*	Florida/New Hampshire	0.992*	Illinois/Ohio	0.952*	Arizona/Iowa	0.894*
Idaho/Nebraska	0.968*	New Hampshire/New Jersey	0.991*	Texas/Utah	0.950*	Florida/Wisconsin	0.891*
Hawaii/Idaho	0.968*	Connecticut/New Mexico	0.991*	Arkansas/South Dakota	0.949*		
Maryland/Massachusetts	0.965*						

Note:

*Indicates that the bivariate correlation of statewide bank ROAs is statistically significant at least at the 5 percent risk level. Small banks have total assets of less than $100 million; medium banks have assets of $100 million to $1 billion, while large banks report total assets of over $1 billion.

Source: Calculations of return on assets (ROA) by the author based on Call Reports and Income Statements provided by the Federal Deposit Insurance Corporation for the 1985–93 period.

states time to adjust their tax structures to avoid huge future losses in tax revenues.

Alert interstate bankers today will assess the *tax consequences* of their proposed expansion strategies *before* additional acquisitions are attempted. This means studying carefully the specific terms of local tax laws and applying for local tax abatements wherever these are available. It also means targeting banks in states where workers' compensation insurance and unemployment taxes are relatively low or can be lowered through legitimate means. For example, some states will allow a bank with low compensation or unemployment tax rates in its home state to carry over these lower assessments into newly entered areas.

The Individual Firm Target: Dimensions of Financial Performance that Characterize Interstate Acquired Banks

Once a state, city, or region is selected as an acquisition target, interstate banking organizations must select particular banks within that locality as possible acquisition targets. Bankers who focus on individual banking firms as possible acquisitions tend to look at the following features of a promising target institution (many of which are summarized in table 6.9):

1. Substantial capital base with adequate-to-strong ratios of equity capital to total assets and to risk-exposed assets, which reduces the necessity for immediately raising new capital to support a merger or acquisition.

2. Strong actual profit performance or above-average profit potential if new management and operating policies can be put into place successfully.

3. A relatively high proportion of core (low interest-sensitive or loyal) deposits held by the acquisition target.

4. A market position or niche suggesting strong future demand for the bank's most profitable services (especially loans), which often is associated with superior locations of branch offices and a favorable reputation or image in the local area, so that the acquiring institution gains immediate access to a favorable local reputation and market standing.

5. Complementarity in management goals and objectives as well as in product focus between the acquirer and the acquired banking firm.

6. Whether the proposed bank target opens up new market areas (for market extension acquisitions and mergers) not previously served by the acquiring banking company.

Table 6.9
Evaluating a Potential Bank Acquisition Target

ASSESSMENT OF THE TARGET BANK'S MARKET AREA

- Recent growth (at least the last ten years) in total area deposits, loans, personal income, bank debits, retail and wholesale sales, new business franchises, unemployment, average hourly compensation (wage) rate, and utility connections.
- Number and relative sizes of financial-service competitors (including banks, credit unions, savings and loans, security brokers, and finance companies).
- Financial and physical condition of local streets, highways, schools, and city and county government facilities.
- State and local rates for income, franchise, property, as well as unemployment taxes and workers' compensation insurance and the possible availability of tax abatements.
- Profitability, growth, and loan-quality records of other depository institutions serving the same market area.
- Current population estimates and population projections for at least two decades into the future along with census data on the employment mix, population age distribution, and family incomes in the local area.

ASSESSMENT OF THE TARGET BANKING FIRM

- Most recent profitability or earnings track record (for at least ten years, if available) measured by return on assets, return on equity capital, net interest margin, net operating margin, and earnings per share of common equity.
- Risk exposure analysis (for at least ten years, if available) covering the track record of net loan losses and recoveries, equity capital, subordinated debt capital, variance of after-tax net income, classified loans, examiner ratings, core deposit volume, and rate of growth.
- Evaluation of physical facilities: current condition and location relative to competing depository institutions serving the same market area and whether any duplication of facilities exists.
- Evaluation of management quality as reflected in examiner ratings, personnel records, educational backgrounds, salary structure and benefits, quality of internal planning documents, and development and marketing of new services.

---

7. Whether the proposed affiliated bank promises the acquirer access to new services or better service delivery systems (e.g., First Union's recent action to acquire First Fidelity and thereby absorb a much-improved security brokerage business).

8. Whether the proposed bank acquisition promises substantial

cost savings due to the elimination of duplicate facilities and personnel and possesses competent management.

9. Whether the bank or banking company that is the target can be acquired without paying too high a price to the target's current shareholders. (This may have happened, for example, in the 1996 announced purchase of Boatmen's Bancshares by NationsBank for $8.7 billion in cash and stock. NationsBank promised to pay Boatmen's shareholders a premium of 40 percent over the market value of Boatmen's stock. In the $750 million acquisition of Citizens Bancorp of Laurel, Maryland by Crestar Financial Corp. of Richmond in which Crestar offered Citizens' shareholders a whopping 53 percent premium over market value).

The foregoing list is similar in certain respects to that developed in a recent study by Richard Sullivan and Kenneth Spong (1996) of the Kansas City Federal Reserve Bank. These economists examined banks acquired across state lines during the years 1985 to 1987. Finding that some interstate companies exhibited superior performance than others, Sullivan and Spong recommended that banking companies interested in successful interstate operations should:

1. acquire banks with a strong presence in their local loan markets and work to hold this position by pursuing moderate loan growth;

2. be cautious about moving out of traditional business and consumer lending roles into higher-risk lending areas;

3. pursue high credit standards and avoid sacrificing credit quality simply to increase total loans;

4. stress earnings rather than asset growth, with particular attention to protecting an acquired bank's net interest margins and not placing too much reliance upon fee (noninterest) income;

5. acquire banks that are effective at controlling operating expenses and move toward lower overhead costs by improving employee productivity; and

6. avoid the presumption that a high acquisition price or a rash of nearby acquisitions guarantees that any acquisition in the same area will necessarily be successful.

Sullivan and Spong observe that interstate bank expansion poses more challenges than intrastate banking used to because, for certain kinds of interstate acquisitions, management must face completely *new* markets where knowledge of customers and competitors is more limited.

The motivations (goals and objectives) for interstate acquisitions of banks are not the same for all acquirers, as noted recently by John W. Spiegel, chief financial officer for Sun Trust banks of Atlanta, and Alan Gart, professor of business at Nova Southeastern University in Fort Lauderdale, Florida (1996). These two authorities in the field recently predicted that the number of U.S. banks would decline by at least 25 percent by the end of the 1990s. Spiegel and Gart see the current consolidation and restructuring to be driven by (a) banking and thrift failures in the 1970s and 1980s; (b) deregulation of the industry by government; (c) more lenient merger guidelines; (d) rising deposit and labor costs; (e) the desire for greater product-line and geographic diversification; (f) changing technology of financial service production and delivery; and (g) a search for revenue growth in an increasingly competitive financial marketplace. Spiegel and Gart classify the bank mergers and acquisitions in the 1990s as falling into four broad categories:

1. *in-market consolidations* (such as the $3.6 billion Fleet/Shawmut national merger announced in February 1995), which allow reduction of duplicate facilities (primarily in the form of branches and back-office processing units);

2. *market extension acquisitions* (such as the First Chicago/NBD merger announced in July 1995 at just over $5 billion and NationsBank Corp.'s $8.7 billion acquisition of Boatmen's BancShares Inc. of St. Louis announced in 1996), which bring together leaders in different markets and geographic regions, bridging the gaps between traditional markets and bringing existing service expertise into new geographic areas, thus offering increased revenue potential;

3. *mergers of equals* (such as Chemical Bank and Chase Manhattan), in which each partner makes a major contribution to the combined entity, and substantial expense reductions may occur, particularly in eliminating duplicative facilities; and

4. *business line extensions* (such as Mellon Bank's purchase of Dreyfus Corporation), which promote financial-services diversification and are often motivated by a desire to generate more fee income and help stabilize a consolidated banking organization's overall revenue flows.

The authors believe that most bank mergers of the future will be of the "in-market" type in order to gain greater efficiency vis-à-vis expense reductions and less duplication. This is not unreasonable given the impact of new information technology in broadening markets so that more competitors are swept into the same market areas and the number of desirable independent banking firms available for acquisition decreases. Spiegel and Gart see sustained growth in earnings along with portfolio quality (controlled risk exposure) as the keys to future dividend growth and stock price appreciation. Many bankers will seek that sustained growth potential in new markets and new products developed through carefully planned and integrated withinstate and out-of-state acquisitions In their view, winning banks are likely to be those that can leverage their distribution networks and provide the greatest number of products and services across the widest customer base in an efficient manner.

One prominent example of a recent interstate acquisition of the market extension variety was the acquisition of National Westminster Bank PLC by Fleet Financial Group in December 1995. Fleet was based predominantly in New England (with headquarters in Rhode Island), with smaller Fleet units operating in upstate New York and Long Island. National Westminster, in contrast, owned 330 branch offices in the New York City area and in New Jersey. Thus, the Fleet-Natwest combination served to fill in a major gap in Fleet's geographic span by adding office facilities in central New York and the state of New Jersey. In contrast, Fleet had agreed to a merger earlier in 1995 with Shawmut National, increasing consolidation in the New England area, where it was already well represented, but opening up the possibility of cost savings from the elimination of duplicate facilities (especially overlapping branch offices and staff).

Even where acquisitions involve banks serving much the same trade territory (in-market consolidations), banks with differing product mixes may come together to increase the revenue and market dominance of the combined organization that emerges as a result of a merger. A good example of such a transaction occurred in December 1995 when the Bank of Boston agreed to pay $2 billion for Bay Banks Inc., a strong retail banking company serving predominantly eastern Massachusetts. Bay Banks appeared to offer the Bank of Boston superior deposit-generating power as a result of its approximately one thousand ATMs, telebanking operations, and supermarket branches.

Most interstate bankers seem to be driven in their cross-border ventures by a search for what they believe are *undervalued* acquisition targets. That is, individual banks or bank holding companies that the market (as reflected in the current stock price per share) has priced too low for the amount of risk and earnings potential they contain. Interstate companies frequently believe that they possess the analytical skills necessary to identify those target banks that the capital markets as a whole have underestimated in terms of future earning power. They typically look for target banks that possess some or all of the following financial profiles:

- relatively low ratios of total loans to total assets compared to other banks of comparable size in the same market area, indicating substantial underutilized lending capacity and, therefore, greater future loan-revenue potential;

- relatively low ratios of total operating expenses to total operating revenues, indicating a well-managed bank, or, alternatively, a bank displaying a relatively high operating expense to revenue ratio but in which new management can substantially reduce future operating costs through automation, staff reductions, branch closings, and other cost-saving actions;

- relatively high ratios of cash assets and investment portfolio assets to total assets that acquiring management can shift into higher-yielding loans and other income-generating service activities by replacing relatively cautious managers and shareholders with more aggressive managers and owners;

- relatively low ratios of problem loans relative to the total loan portfolio as compared to neighboring banks, indicating a high-quality loan portfolio upon which new management can build an expanded loan case, accepting somewhat greater risk but also gaining expanded loan revenues and loan-servicing fees;

- relatively high returns on total assets (ROA) but relatively low returns on equity capital (ROE), suggesting a target bank that has relied heavily upon equity capital supplied by its stockholders but could profitably use increased debt in its capital structure in order to lever up shareholder returns; and

- relatively high ratios of checkable deposits and savings accounts in supporting bank assets, suggesting the potential availability of low-cost funding sources in the target bank's relevant market area that could be profitably employed in the various market areas served by the acquiring interstate firm.

CONCLUSION

Today interstate banking is a search for new markets, new service opportunities, and "undervalued" depository institutions. To be successful, interstate bankers must develop new analytical tools that can identify accurately both superior target markets and superior target banking firms. This is no small challenge in a nation with thousands of relatively small banking firms who possess widely varying prospects for the future. A well-formed interstate banking strategy must rest on quality management and a thorough understanding of the changing market for financial services and the changing economic interests of bank customers. There is no one dimension of a market or of a potential target banking firm that dominates all the rest. Rather, those states and regions and individual banking firms with the most stable deposit bases, substantial population and personal income growth prospects with moderate tax and insurance rates, the greatest potential for loan and service income, and the strongest outlook for quality credit accounts appear to be the most likely target areas and institutions for future interstate bank expansion.

CHAPTER 7

The Consequences of Interstate Banking for the Public, the Regulatory Community, and Banks Themselves

Many observers expect the American banking industry to consolidate rapidly, paralleling changes now underway in Europe, where economic integration has become a powerful restructuring force for banking and many other industries. If this expectation is met, a generation from now the industry's population may be no more than three or four thousand, resulting in a banking system closer to the one that exists today in Canada, Germany, Great Britain, and selected other countries around the globe.

Whether or not the foregoing numbers are close to the mark, several structural trends currently underway in America's banking industry are likely to continue for the foreseeable future. These include:

1. continuing concentration of assets and deposits in the largest U.S. banking companies on a nationwide basis (though little change is likely to take place in service concentration in most cities and small towns across the United States);

2. further expansion in the numbers of customer-service facilities, but a change in the channels of service distribution toward more automated and semiautomated facilities, so that customers do more of their own routine banking transactions;

3. more employee layoffs in an industry that currently employs about 1.7 million people as merging banking firms seek to

reduce needless duplication in facilities and personnel and the American banking industry continues its drift toward a more capital intensive, and less labor intensive, service industry;

4. greater pressures upon hundreds of small banks (especially those below $500 million to $1 billion in total assets) to compete more aggressively or leave the industry. To survive, small banks in the United States must grapple with the rising cost of production and service delivery innovations, address the need for larger-scale advertising programs in order to reach a more mobile and more widely dispersed customer base, and face the increasing technical demands of tomorrow's high-speed payments and information systems.

In some respects at least this consolidation trend in American banking will be a *positive* development. It should make regulation and control of the industry easier and more efficient with fewer banks for regulators to monitor. Government policymakers will be able to communicate their goals and changing rules faster and more completely to CEOs and boards of directors of the banking firms under their jurisdiction. It may also make the surviving banking firms more resistant to the ebb and flow of the business cycle so that there are fewer bank failures, increasing the confidence of the public in the ultimate stability of the banking system and improving the efficiency and lowering the costs associated with making payments and transferring financial information. Moreover, a consolidated banking system may lead to greater efficiency and less cost in scarce resources in transferring and storing financial information and in making payments for purchases of goods and services.

However, the American banking industry's current consolidation trend will not be without cost, either to the industry or to the public. There may well be less sensitivity to local service needs in hundreds of smaller cities and towns, thus hastening the movement of businesses and population toward central cities and metropolitan areas. Very few multiple-office banks seem to know how to provide personalized services or how to develop close, long-term relationships with their household and small-business customers as smaller banks do.

As banking becomes less personalized, it is also likely to present most customers with fewer service options due to *increased consolidation* of the industry into much larger and fewer separately owned individual banking firms. The typical customer—business, government, or individual—will face fewer alternative sources of supply (even though there is also evidence that few households really shop around for financial services). It becomes *imperative*, then, that federal authorities—the banking agencies and the Department of Justice—work even harder to evaluate the competitive effects (especially the potential damage to competition in the "potentially most damaged market" where individuals and small businesses seek out financial services). Those proposed cross-state mergers and acquisitions that seem to have a significant adverse impact on competition must be opposed aggressively if the economies of scale (cost) benefits of banking consolidation are to come through to the consumer rather than be drowned in abusive anticompetitive behavior.

The concept of what is the "potentially most damaged market" may need to be expanded to include businesses and individuals who trade in markets slightly broader than a single community. The problem with interstate banking is that whole regions, encompassing neighboring towns and cities, gradually become more concentrated over time. Customers denied access to financial services at reasonable cost in one local community travel to another community, only to be confronted with offices of the same banks. This is particularly worrisome for small and medium businesses. This sector above all others seems to need the most attention from the Justice Department and the banking agencies. Indeed, consumers (individuals and families) seem to have attracted more service options in recent years due to the rise of family-oriented nonbank financial-service providers (including credit unions, savings associations, security brokers and dealers, and finance and leasing companies). For small and medium businesses, on the other hand, the structure of the supply side of their financial-services marketplace appears to be little changed from a decade or more ago.

Interstate banking tends to tie markets together, so that banking oligopoly emerges—few banks offering essentially the same services. In this kind of marketplace, bankers soon become aware of their mutual interdependence as they square off to face one another in one local neighborhood after another. In such an environment, "understandings" about market shares and pricing terms are not inevitable, but they do become more feasible and, therefore, more likely. Thus, regulatory supervision of the merger and acquisition market becomes more, not less, important as interstate banking reaches out to capture a major share of American banking. This is particularly true in the wake of the hundreds of bank and savings and loan failures during the 1980s and early 1990s. It is also true because of what research evidence has shown about the general lack of public (as opposed to private) benefits from interstate bank consolidations. If interstate mergers and acquisitions do not, on balance, advance the public interest, then close scrutiny of any mergers and acquisitions that are proposed for possible damage to competition becomes all the more relevant. This is not to say that interstate banking makes no positive contributions to the nation and to local communities, for, indeed, if interstate banking focuses capital toward its most productive, highest return uses, then the public must be regarded as better off because the nation's scarce resources are being employed more efficiently with less waste.

Moreover, some depositors will lose a portion of their FDIC-supplied deposit insurance protection as consolidation spreads across the banking industry. This will happen, as seen in chapter 4, because customers with separate deposits in each of two banks that merge, while qualifying for up to $200,000 in protection before a merger, will, after the merger, only receive a maximum of $100,000 in insurance protection, unless they can suitably restructure the ownership of their deposits through the establishment of trust accounts and other legal devices.

However, be careful about prematurely writing small banks out of the industry and assuming that they will ultimately be victims of interstate banking. Consolidation will continue, but hundreds, if not thousands, of smaller banks can survive and do well (that is, remain among the industry's leaders in rates of return and operating efficiency). True, the smaller half of the industry's population will probably continue to lose market share (measured by its percentage of total industry assets) due to the inroads of new communications technology and the effectiveness of nonbank competitors (especially mutual funds and security dealers). Moreover, as both Jackson (1992) and Levonian (1995) have recently observed, important segments of the market for banking services are becoming national in scope (including the markets for savings instruments, residential mortgage loans, and credit-card services). Banks of all sizes must change and adapt to this market-broadening trend; however, this does *not* mean that all small banks must become large banks. Many, if not most, of the new services and communications links that smaller banks will need in the future can be supplied through one of the oldest institutions in the industry—the correspondent banking system, in which larger banks provide essential services to smaller banks in return for fees or deposits. The industry's leading correspondent banks still seek to expand their links to smaller institutions as an important source of fee income that flows directly to their bottom line. Moreover, bankers' banks, which provide services to many smaller banks, received expanded powers and greater future opportunities for expansion with passage of the Riegle-Neal interstate banking bill in 1994.

Where correspondent and bankers' banks are unwilling or unable to supply new services and communications channels to smaller banking firms at reasonable cost, several nonbank corporations are eagerly waiting on the sidelines to carve out a substantial share of the interbank service market. Two prominent examples are Microsoft Corporation and Intuit, Inc., who have recently invaded the home and office banking market and are offering banks of all sizes dial-up services to customers using Microsoft's Money or Intuit's Quicken—both highly popular personal finance programs. In the spring of 1996 Microsoft announced a new browser program on the Internet that will assist customers trying to pay bills, transfer funds, and carry out other financial transactions by reaching their banks' Web sites on the Internet. In effect, the new Microsoft program will turn the World Wide

Web into an automated teller machine, comparable to the more than one hundred thousand ATMs already established across the United States in stores, malls, and other customer-convenient locations. Continuing competition among computer companies should continue to lower the price of electronic service linkages, opening many of the newest service delivery vehicles even to the smallest banks in the industry. The Internet may also aid smaller banks needing to raise capital in the future as Web pages are created to sell small amounts of stock directly to investors, bypassing investment banking houses and the securities exchanges.

Banking in the future will follow and, in some respects, contribute to the great demographic and social trends that seem to be refashioning American society itself. The continuing flow of business enterprises and consumers to the western and southeastern portions of the nation will cause banking's most aggressive competitors to move the industry's focus and resources toward the new, unfolding markets within the United States and to newer and more promising opportunities abroad as well, including the expanding NAFTA trade area, the remainder of Central and South America, China and the western Pacific, and both Eastern and Western Europe. The expertise that American banks have developed and sharpened to a fine point in reaching out to domestic households and small businesses will be exploited in these more distant arenas, which offer tremendous revenue potential to those banking companies able to achieve the size, financial strength, and expertise to reach into the most promising markets.

LEADING PLAYERS IN THE DEVELOPING NATIONAL BANKING SYSTEM

The leading players have already begun to emerge in this developing struggle for U.S. banking's growth and survival. They include:

- *NationsBank,* which ranked twenty-fourth in total assets in 1985 but rose dramatically to third place with assets totaling almost $190 billion by 1995; *NationsBank* then held onto fourth place (moving ahead of J. P. Morgan and Co.) in 1996 with the announced acquisition of Boatmen's Bancshares, Inc., moving up to about $230 billion in total assets;
- *First Union Corp.,* which ranked only forty-fifth in asset size in 1985 but had firmly grasped sixth place in 1995 with close to $124 billion in assets in the wake of a merger with First Fidelity Corp.;
- *BankOne,* which soared from forty-first to tenth in aggregate assets between 1985 and 1995, when it held nearly $90 billion in assets under management;

- *Chase/Chemical Bancorp.*, which will rank number one in resources when its latest merger is completed and hold close to $300 billion in total assets, whereas Chemical ranked sixth in 1983 while Chase Manhattan ranked third;

- *First Chicago Corp.*, ranking eighth in 1995 from eleventh a decade earlier with control over nearly $120 billion in aggregate assets and may move up to seventh in total assets when the planned acquisition of Detroit's NBD Bancorp. is complete, making First Chicago a dominant force in the Midwest;

- *Wells Fargo Corporation*, which joins the nation's leaders in efficient production and delivery of services and, thanks to its recent acquisition of First Interstate Banks, has one of the most stable deposit bases in the United States;

- *BankAmerica*, whose industry rank held steady at number two in both 1985 and 1995 while managing close to $225 billion in assets; and

- *Fleet Financial Group* (Providence), which may rank as high as eighth overall because its most recently announced mergers (including Shawmut National Corp. of Boston) would propel that New England–based company to nearly $120 billion in total assets.

Among the most likely takeover targets among other U.S. banking leaders today are Bankers Trust New York Corp., Key Corp. (which ranked among the industry's earnings leaders in 1995); Bank of Boston Corp. (another national leader in earnings in 1995); National City Corp.; UJB Financial of Princeton; Huntington Bancshares of Columbus; Mellon Bank of Pittsburgh (also a leading company nationwide in net earnings); BT Financial in Johnstown; U.S. Bancorp. in Oregon; Comerica Inc. of Detroit; Barnett Banks Inc. (Florida's last major independent); Hibernia Bank in New Orleans; Crestar Financial Corp. of Richmond; Mercantile Bancorp in Missouri; Old Kent Financial Corp. of Grand Rapids; Deposit Guaranty Corp.; Meridian Bancorp. of Reading, Pennsylvania; Colonial BancGroup; West One Bancorp in Idaho; Deposit Guaranty of Jackson, Mississippi; and Colonial BancGroup of Montgomery, Alabama.

These most recent acquirers and likely acquisition targets seem to reflect a common concern among today's leaders in American banking about an ongoing "revenue crunch." At many large American banks, revenue growth has been relatively flat for several years running. Bankers have come to fear further declines in their market shares as nonbank financial-service firms and the finance affiliates of leading industrial corporations like Ford Motor Company, General Electric Corp., and General Motors offer greater competition and tear away large chunks of banking's traditional customer base. Competition is especially intense today between bank and nonbank companies for the asset-based financing of midsize and emerging businesses and for a greater share of the market for consumer credit cards. Both of these product lines offer high potential profit margins for those banking firms that can achieve greater service volume while tightly controlling production costs and capping losses due to customer default and fraud.

At the same time rapid technological change in the storage and movement of financial information via satellite, cellular telephone, and computer networks is rapidly expanding the geographic boundaries of both domestic and foreign banking markets. More mobile customers demand immediate access to payments, savings, and credit accounts and seek out those banking firms that offer greater transactional convenience and rapid credit decisions. Banks that can offer speed, reliability, low transactions cost, and full market coverage will have a decisive edge in the financial-services marketplace of the twenty-first century.

The changing technology of banking is bound to make reaching across state lines to snare new customers much easier in the future, even without an interstate banking law. And banks in a competitive financial marketplace seem to have little hesitation about taking quick advantage of new service production and delivery methods. The World Wide Web, for example, has attracted widespread attention in the industry. Not only are home pages on the Web common for many banks of all sizes, but direct Web service delivery is a rapidly developing option. One of the most interesting recent examples was posted by PNC Bank Corporation of Pittsburgh in the summer of 1996. PNC's World Wide Web site was designed to allow around-the-clock access to "customized banking"—a personalized range of services—and to loan calculators. To protect customer privacy, the new PNC System establishes a protocol that encrypts data and verifies server and clients' computer systems through Netscape. Customers can, in effect, create their own "home page" to serve their specialized service needs. PNC's Web site also advertises the availability of several corporate banking services—treasury management, leasing, capital markets access, institutional trust, and liquidity management. Then in September of 1996 International Business Machines, Inc. (IBM) and 15 leading banking firms—including PNC, KeyCorp of Cleveland, Mellon Bank of Pittsburgh, and Fleet Financial Group of Boston—announced the creation of a home banking system, labeled The Integrion Financial Network. Among the many services promised by this co-owned IBM-bank system will be remote banking over the Internet, access to personal financial software, telephone banking, and the availability of on-line consumer transactions.

MANAGEMENT ISSUES IN INTERSTATE BANKING

The unfolding of interstate banking will present significant new challenges for *bank managers* at all levels. The key issues are *coordination* and *communication*, for interstate banks are generally among the most complicated and intricate of all financial-service firms, with multiple offices and affiliated companies spread out over the landscape. The largest interstate banks serve a wide diversity of states and regions, each with somewhat unique credit and other service needs. Unless management works aggressively to improve the internal flow of information in *both* directions, from senior management down to branch managers and staff and from branch offices up to senior management, the interstate firm will not be able to react quickly enough to changing conditions in the marketplace and to emerging internal problems. Problem areas may fester and grow before senior management is fully aware of the difficulties and can develop and implement effective solutions.

Coordination and communications problems have led several leading banks (for example, Barnett Banks and BancOne of Ohio) to develop a more *decentralized* organizational form. Local managers are given greater latitude to identify local problems and develop and implement solutions that deal specifically with local problems. Local managers are also allowed to make final decisions on larger loans so that customers can receive their funds more quickly. Contrary to popular opinion, such an approach is *less*, not more, costly than greater centralization of authority and decision making, as described in chapter 5 where a recent study by Chicago Federal Reserve economist Dr. William C. Hunter (1995) was reviewed. Contrary to those who believe strongly in centralization, Hunter found *only one* instance in which centralizing bank functions reduced costs—specifically in consolidating so-called back-office operations—for example, accounting, advertising, and computing functions.

Decentralization means empowerment of local management and staff to be assertive and creative and to respond more quickly to customer requests. It gives local managers the feeling of being "in charge" when dealing with the needs of local communities and in preserving service relationships with long-standing customers while "going the extra mile" to win new ones. Otherwise, smaller local banks, who do have the flexibility to respond quickly to their local customer needs, will steal away those customers fed up with the bureaucracy and delays that may prevail in some interstate systems where all the decisions that really matter are referred to personnel outside the local area.

Management must also be alert to the need for new *capital* as new acquisitions are made and new branches are set up or acquired. Expansion through the construction or acquisition of new facilities is one of the most expensive steps bankers can take, particularly as banking becomes more computerized and its equipment needs grow commensurately. Capital, mostly supplied by the bank's owners, becomes the foundation upon which a bank expands geographically. However, capital is usually a banker's most expensive funding source and takes time to raise because of security registration requirements and the need to find the right moment to approach the capital market for funds.

In the past, before the decade of the 1980s, bankers could often wait a while before having to come up with additional capital if their capital-to-asset ratios fell due to the rapid expansion of their loans and other assets. There were no or few requirements spelling out specific minimum amounts of capital for each bank. Most banks were let alone if their capital ratios were roughly comparable to neighboring institutions. Since there was a general trend toward falling capital ratios for more than half a century before the new capital standards of the 1980s and 1990s were put in place, bankers could argue that their banks' falling capital ratios were not out of line with the rest of the industry.

This lenient public policy regarding bank capital requirements is no longer in force, however, because of the adoption of new capital requirements under the terms of the 1988 Basle Agreement on International Bank Capital Standards and the passage in the United States of the FDIC Improvement Act of 1991. These historic documents have made *capital* the centerpiece of current banking regulation. The new capital requirements have become a critical benchmark for banks bent on interstate expansion because only "adequately capitalized" banks normally are permitted to make interstate acquisitions or branch across state lines. In light of these recent developments, financial managers of interstate organizations must become more aware of innovations in new fund-raising instruments and knowledgeable about foreign markets where capital can sometimes be raised less expensively than from domestic sources.

Interstate expansion via acquisition likewise raises management concerns about how to mesh what were formerly independent banking institutions into consolidated companies. The management of successful interstate companies must work constantly to improve their skills in identifying potentially profitable acquisitions and finding promising sites for new facilities across state lines. This means that bank managers must know more about the dimensions and character of local economies in distant states—a subject about which they may know very little today. They must also learn how to evaluate the performance of target banks and how that performance might impact the banking units already a part of the acquiring company. Management must be able to assess the competitive environment that potential target banks operate in and figure out ways to improve bank performances in those markets that appear to be attractive for future entry. Interstate bankers must also be alert for hidden costs that often lie inside target banks and branches—for example, aging and outdated facilities that will have to be replaced or upgraded, management and staff that will require retraining, and current bank service locations that no longer lie along the main pathway of community growth and expansion.

Moreover, acquisitions of local banks often raise havoc with customer and employee goodwill. Managers and staff of targeted firms usually fear for their jobs, both immediately and in the long run, wondering if and when they may be phased out—victims of downsizing and retooling. Planned communication is essential between old and new management and owners, giving all employees a chance to ask questions about their current and future roles, understand the goals and objectives of the new owners, and receive reassurances that the acquirer's management is concerned about their questions and especially about their reactions to change. As acquisitions are made across state lines, managers will frequently need to make adjustments in personnel policies and employee compensation schedules to insure that both old and new employees are compensated fairly when performing the same kinds of tasks. Otherwise, a sense of "them" versus "us" can set in following a merger or acquisition, with scores of disaffected managers and staff members choosing either to leave (and take their valuable knowledge and experience with them) or to work defensively in an effort to protect their own positions rather than working aggressively as a team to fulfill the goals of the new consolidated company.

Equally important, management must learn how to deal with the *concerns of customers*, particularly the customers of the bank or banks being acquired. Several recent mergers have been accompanied by the creation of customer "hot lines" to answer the questions that most customers have about a new bank merger:

- Can I still use my old checks and old ATM and credit cards?
- Whom do I call when my checking account has problems?
- Will any service fees or hours of service access be changed?
- Is the local branch where I trade going to be closed?
- What will happen to my loan relationship with the bank?
- Can I still deal with the same bank staff as before or must I divulge my personal information to new employees whom I don't even know (and, by implication, don't yet trust)?
- Will it take me longer now to get approval on a loan?
- Will all decisions about service have to be referred to the home office?
- Is the bank pursuing this merger because it is in trouble and may fail? What exactly is the reason for this most recent change of ownership?

It is questions and concerns like these that often have led the customers of merging banks to leave, seeking friendlier and faster service delivery from competitors. This is probably one of the reasons interstate banks do *not* have an impressive record of defending and expanding their market shares in many local communities; in fact, many of these organizations have a track record of declining market shares of local deposits and loans.

Branch managers must be trained to show the same care and concern for the unique service needs of local businesses and families that the managers and staff of small, locally based banks often display. They must learn how to dispel the widespread perception that big banks (particularly those banks controlled by out-of-state shareholders) care little about smaller businesses and families as customers and prefer dealing only with the largest corporations. Usually this change of attitude requires some degree of decentralization within the acquiring organization, letting local management and staff make more of those decisions that directly impact the customer. In addition, acquiring management must work to reduce employee turnover so that customers are not confronted frequently by bank employees they do not know and may not trust. These steps are particularly critical in dealing with households and small businesses, which are being formed as a rapid rate today and offer the prospect of substantial bank profits if services are priced correctly and loans are carefully managed to keep risk within acceptable limits.

Interstate banks are gradually awakening to the notion that what happens at the local level—in each branch office and community served—dramatically affects the banks' performance and long-run success. Several of the industry's leading interstate banks are doing some or all of the following activities:

- encouraging branch managers to become active community members, joining service clubs and community causes and visiting different parts of the local area rather than remaining behind the office desk

- inviting community leaders to serve on bank boards of directors, either in an advisory capacity or as full-fledged stockholders

- forming community development corporations to improve local housing and support the development of new businesses

- setting up consumer advisory panels selected from the list of current bank customers to evaluate the bank's services, facilities, and employee friendliness

- offering education classes regularly to current and potential new customers, explaining how to apply for and qualify for a loan and what the bank has to offer in the way of new services

On the surface at least, these seem like time-consuming initiatives with few tangible rewards were it not for the fact that banking *is* truly a "relationship business." Customer goodwill and trust is vital to the successful management of a bank because all banks sell virtually the same services. However, trust and customer goodwill must be earned over time by aggressively reaching out to local communities and cannot be achieved without a substantial commitment of both time and treasure.

THE CONSEQUENCES FOR THE PUBLIC AND FOR REGULATION OF INTERSTATE BANK EXPANSION

Hopefully, interstate banking will have positive outcomes for the public it serves. This section describes some of the most hoped-for outcomes.

Increased Service Availability

Interstate banking's growth should expand the menu of services available to most Americans, particularly those living in larger cities and those who regularly cross state lines on their way to work, shopping, school, and recreation. Today the number of bank facilities—including full-service branches and limited-service automated facilities—is increasing, with more than 110,000 ATMs and close to sixty-five thousand full-service branches in the United States alone.

However, there are telltale signs that suggest a gradual decline in the number of bank-operated and bank-maintained facilities in future years. As San Francisco Federal Reserve economists Fred Furlong and Gary Zimmerman (1995) note, the number of banking facilities per capita in California—currently the nation's largest consumer-oriented (retail) banking market—has been in steady decline since 1985. For example, between 1991 and 1993 the number of California banking offices fell from 5,555 to 4,411—a drop of close to 20 percent. If California's current trend in banking offices is a forecast for American banking nationwide, consolidation eventually may lead to substantially fewer banking offices as well as fewer banking companies. The key question then may become whether bank customers will find less convenience in accessing bank services or will simply do more of their own banking through the Internet, home and office computer links, and the telephone, and, therefore, will have less need for bank-supplied service delivery facilities.

Not all customer groups will necessarily be well served in the new consolidated banking industry that is emerging across the United States, however. One group in particular—the small business customer—may be a casualty of a rapidly consolidating banking system, as noted in chapters 4 and 5. A recent study by Federal Reserve Bank of Kansas City economist William Keeton (1995) finds that some types of banks—including such fast-growing industry groups as holding-company-affiliated banks and interstate organizations—tend to devote a smaller proportion of their deposits to small businesses customers, suggesting that the continuing consolidation of smaller banks into larger, multiple-office units may reduce the access of smaller businesses to loans unless steps are taken by government regulatory agencies, which enforce the rules of the competitive game, to insure that local financial-service markets remain fully competitive.

Be cautious, however, in moving too hastily to condemn larger banking firms, because multiple-office banks may tend to acquire banks that make fewer small business loans rather than deliberately discouraging such loans once a bank is acquired by these organizations. Moreover, as noted in chapter 5, if multiple-office banks are safer, they may provide *a more reliable credit supply to small businesses,* even if they ultimately make fewer numbers of loans to emerging firms.

Competitive Pricing of Banking Services

The size and scope of the impact of interstate banking on competition for financial services is particularly difficult to read at this time. On the one hand, there will be many fewer banks in most urban markets as U.S. banking continues to consolidate, but each surviving financial institution should be more aggressive in the quantity of services it provides, if not in service quality. Interstate banks often appear to raise the prices of their services over time, particularly following a new acquisition, but this trend toward higher service fees may be due, in part, to their superior ability to determine their true service production and delivery costs, and their belief that these costs should be passed on to the ultimate service user.

There is at least anecdotal evidence that bank service fees *are* rising, particularly those fees attached to checking accounts and savings deposits. A survey of 271 banks located in twenty-five states and Washington, D.C., conducted over the April 1993 to April 1995 period by the U.S. Public Interest Research Group, found that the average fee associated with interest-bearing checking accounts rose 11 percent over the 1993–95 period, or about twice the rate of inflation in consumer prices, closely followed by regular non-interest-bearing checking accounts, whose average service fee rose 10 percent over the same time period. Maintenance fees on savings accounts rose about 9 percent, while ATM fees increased between 6 and 7 percent, depending on whether local or national ATM networks were used by the customer. Moreover, this same study group found that the average monthly balance a customer must hold to avoid paying any checkable deposit fees climbed about 30 percent to more than $1,200 during the 1993–95 period. Worse still, the Public Interest Research Group reports that the largest banks posted the highest deposit fees, on average. Among the states reporting the highest deposit fees were Florida, Illinois, Maryland, and North Carolina. At least three of these states have served as the home state for industry-leading interstate banking companies.

In fairness to interstate banks and other depository institutions, however, it must be pointed out that operating costs (particularly the cost of new processing equipment and facilities and training personnel to use them) have increased significantly. Moreover, checking-account crime is also on the rise as the number of fraudulent and insufficient-funds checks continues to grow. Deregulation and increasing consumer sensitivity to the prices posted by competitors has generally resulted in more volatile deposits, which also increases bank costs. Then, too, many banks have recently been offering customers free or low-cost software (such as Microsoft Money and Quicken) to encourage at-home banking.

Thus, service fees have recently tended to rise at most banks, both large and small, and not just at interstate institutions. Costs and risks appear to be driving forces behind the ongoing thrust toward higher and higher bank service fees. Nor can it be said for sure that future service fees will be still higher than they are today. The rapidly changing technology of information should increase bank employee productivity and lead to lower operating costs per service unit. Service fees could decline as banking, particularly the deposit processing side of the business, becomes more capital intensive and less dependent on human labor to produce and deliver services.

On balance, there is little to say, with confidence, about the likely track that future prices of banking services will take. It is highly probable, however, that there will be a greater variety of banking services and greater transactional convenience for the consumer, even if bank services do cost more.

Greater Bank Safety and Capital Savings

Bank safety should be enhanced because, as interstate banking spreads, individual banks will be less dependent upon a narrow set of local markets. Rather, American banks will be able to bring together regions with widely varying economic profiles and, thereby, stabilize their overall earnings and cash flow. With greater geographic diversification *and* greater diversity of services offered, interstate banks' revenue flows should be less subject to local market fluctuations and there may be less need for large volumes of bank capital to preserve the stability and long-run viability of American banks.

However, it must be stressed that these hoped-for outcomes are, at this point, only conjecture and speculation. Very different outcomes may be found than currently expected from interstate bank expansion in the final analysis, especially in the areas of service pricing and bank safety and soundness. In a regulated industry there is no guarantee that only the lowest cost, most efficient producers will survive. High-cost banks may well be able to coexist in the long run along side more efficient units due to the protective umbrella of government involvement in this high-impact, high-profile industry.

Just as there must be extra caution in believing that interstate banking will yield all the benefits its proponents have promised, people must be realistic about what it is *not* likely to be able to do. In all probability, interstate banking will have little or no impact on the nation's rate of economic growth and development. To be sure, dozens of states during the 1980s and early 1990s voted to join the interstate banking system in the vain hope that new jobs and capital investment would provide an economic boost to their local communities. Nearly two decades later, researchers find scant evidence that the hoped-for economic benefits emerged. There seems little doubt from the body of existing research evidence that the structural forms banks employ to produce and deliver their services—whether holding company or branching-type organizations or whether bank growth takes place via internal capital generation or through mergers—seem to be of minor importance from an economic point of view. Rather, states, regions, and local communities depend for their economic survival on the plentitude or scarcity of natural resources, the quality and speed of communications and transport, the willingness of businesses and individuals to save and invest a significant portion of their incomes, the acceptance by the tax-paying public of the costs of high-quality schools, and the accessibility to the marketplace for the goods and services produced. In short, the *externalities* of interstate banking—what it will do for the rest of the economy and for the public interest—will probably be far less relevant in the real world than will be the *internalities* of the interstate form—what it will do for or to its owners and employees. If, as many authorities believe, interstate banking treats its stockholders and employees well and is innocuous in its impact upon the economy and the public as a whole, it will likely survive and expand gradually into most corners of the nation.

And, while on the subject of what interstate banking cannot or probably will not do, there needs to be firmly put to rest the decades-old claim that interstate banking will drain scarce capital from some local communities, causing them to wither and die, while loanable funds are diverted only to the largest corporations and governments. This fear began in the nineteenth century when branch office powers were first considered and publicly debated and has reared its head again in the era of interstate banking. Interstate banks have shown themselves to be aggressive institutions. Where there is credit demand that seems to promise competitive rates of return, interstate institutions generally will make credit available on reasonably competitive terms. The industry is well aware that draining a community of its deposits without returning a flow of capital to it in the form of loans is economically destructive in the long run and would ultimately threaten the viability of the institution's local branch offices. Research suggests that local deposits and local loans tend to be remarkably alike in volume across both large and small banks, in part because these two oldest of banking services are rarely sold independently of one another. Local deposit growth requires growth in local loans and vice versa. Indeed, the available research evidence to date suggests that it is smaller, more locally focused banks that tend to send a larger percentage of their total funds out of their local areas into national and international securities markets simply as a vehicle for reducing risk exposure in case the local economy crashes. Interstate banks tend to display the highest loan-to-asset ratios in the American banking industry, while small local banks, on average, generally report the lowest loan-asset ratios.

This does *not* mean, however, that interstate banking firms will necessarily expand their lending to all business firms and households. There is still room for concern about how well interstate banks will treat small businesses and respond to their credit needs. Nor does it mean that interstate banks will never find occasions to drain scarce loanable funds away from some of the communities served by their branches, particularly when their largest metropolitan banks face real crises and desperately need new capital. What all this does mean is that interstate banking is, by and large, *profit motivated* and, therefore, in an interstate banking system, credit will be more likely to flow toward those assets with the highest expected returns, in whatever locality or marketplace those most rewarding projects appear to lie.

Furthermore, the trend toward interstate banking in its present form is *not* irreversible or inevitable. The history of banking is also a history of *regulation*; government involvement in what banks do and where they are located is nearly as old as the industry itself, particularly in Europe and the United States. Banks, especially the largest banking firms, generate much fear and apprehension among consumers, who often do not understand the banking business and worry about being ripped off by unscrupulous "money changers."

U.S. history contains numerous examples of banks or bankers becoming the targets of angry mobs and of hasty, punitive regulation traceable to perceived injustices or outright fear of concentrated market power banks seem to possess. If interstate banks turn out to be high-cost, risky service providers and if some of the larger ones begin to fail, new legislation and new regulations are almost inevitable. History has repeatedly demonstrated that governments do not hesitate to intervene in the banking system when the public's savings are threatened or when service availability and pricing run counter to the public's sense of what is fair and reasonable. Bankers are not today, nor have they ever been, free to do exactly what they please. Global competition is too intense in an industry that, increasingly, knows no boundaries to the marketplaces it can and will serve due to advances in information technology and greater customer mobility.

WILL BANKING COSTS REALLY DECLINE?

When the Riegle-Neal interstate banking bill was being debated in the U.S. Congress in 1994, its passage was made more likely by widespread claims that freedom to expand across state lines would make it possible for banking companies to lower their operating costs substantially. It was argued that branch offices are cheaper to operate than a string of separately incorporated full-service banks with separate managements and boards of directors. This popular "cost-saving hypothesis" remains to be convincingly demonstrated, however, because some operating costs may actually increase in a more consolidated banking industry.

If the step toward nationwide branching means greater centralization of authority in home or regional headquarters, the increased costs of communicating decisions within a larger and more complex interstate firm could be high enough to offset other savings that banks may reap through consolidation. Indeed, decentralized banking firms (such as those structured like BankOne of Ohio) may average substantially lower operating costs than highly centralized banking firms, particularly because of their quicker reaction to changing local market conditions. If so, the hoped-for cost savings from interstate bank expansion may evaporate. In that event the future of interstate banking may have to rest upon a different set of pillars (such as reduced failure risk or increased customer convenience) rather than the promise of greater efficiency.

INTERSTATE BANKING IN A LARGER CONTEXT

The positive outcomes from the spread of interstate banking that many people hope for must be tempered with the realization that some things must inevitably be lost. One of these casualties is likely to be the shared authority and responsibility of the federal government and the states over the supervision of the banking system. To many observers, the passage of the Riegle-Neal interstate banking law has seemed like little more than a mere validation of what the states had already carried out when forty-nine of the fifty states passed legislation in the 1980s and 1990s to allow bank holding companies to enter their territory from other states. But, viewed in historical perspective—from the broad sweep of American banking history— the new interstate banking law is a significant departure—some would say, a sharp turn in direction and course—from the century-old tradition of a *dual banking system.*

For well over a hundred years, stretching from the Civil War of the 1860s to the mid-1990s, the parallel existence of both federal and state banking systems seemed essential to protecting the public while encouraging regulatory creativity and innovation. When bankers found one of the two (federal and state) regulatory systems too burdensome, they could switch to the other system, giving up a state charter to apply for the national banking system or vice versa, and retain their competitive edge. U.S. banking history is replete with examples of Congress and the state legislatures vying among themselves for preserving federal and state authority and leveling the playing field for national and state banking systems.

Riegle-Neal, however, is a major step toward a federally dominated banking system. It is by no means the first such step—many authorities would argue that the Bank Merger and Bank Holding Company Acts of the 1950s, 1960s, and 1970s as well as the depository institution deregulation laws of the 1980s were other important steps in the drive toward federal hegemony over American banking, giving the federal government a preeminent position in the decisions of banks to expand their operations and reach into new service markets. But, in these cases, the states retained critical decision-making powers over entry by out-of-state banking organizations and over branching activity and new-bank formations within their borders.

Riegle-Neal, however, is a new story in which the sun is definitely setting for the dual system, at least as a major influence on the bulk of the nation's banking assets and leading banking organizations. True, the states were given a window of opportunity to reject the tide of federal dominance—to "opt out" of the national banking system. But, unlike the past when the states faced no time fuses—they could react at their own speed, within their own frame of reference, Rielge-Neal has confronted the states with unprecedented deadlines—to act before June 1997 or let the new federal system determine the character of local banking. For those states choosing to "opt out"of the national system, their banks face the bitter possibility of running the risk of a drastic decline in the value of banking franchises (licenses) in those states, limiting the options available to their owners to maximize shareholder value. Banks in "opt out" states also face the risk that they will be unable to raise adequate capital, thus placing them in harm's way because of the tougher capital standards now imposed on all federally insured U.S. depository institutions as a result of passage of the FDIC Improvement Act in 1991.

The loss of competition between federal and state bank regulatory systems as a result of the erosion of the American dual banking system could have significant long-run consequences. Competition between federal and state agencies in the past often led to regulatory innovation, usually to gradually freeing the industry from geographic or product-line constraints. With one centralized system there is the danger of rigidifying the regulatory structure because federal regulators may feel less pressure to respond to both banker and public concerns. Of course, regulatory centralization may simplify the process of regulatory and legislative change with only one group of regulators and one legislative body involved instead of fifty or more. How this will actually play out remains to be seen. But there is at least the danger that the United States will move farther toward a lethargic and unresponsive regulatory regime, which would retard the development of American banking and might further decrease banking's declining market share.

One way to avoid further damage to the dual regulatory system is greater cooperation among federal and state agencies. As R. Chris Moore (1996), head of the Banking Supervision and Regulation division at the Federal Reserve Bank of Cleveland, has noted, "effective regulation of interstate banking will require a lot more coordination among the regional Federal Reserve Banks, as well as between the various regulatory agencies" (p. 1). Among the greatest challenges for regulators are preserving the integrity of the dual (state and federal) banking systems so that regulations do not significantly favor one system (such as the federal) over the other. To help avoid federal or state favoritism in regulating U.S. banks the Conference of State Bank Supervisors, the FDIC, and the Federal Reserve System have recently begun to hammer out cooperative agreements—known as *protocols*—to simplify the examination process for banks chartered by the states that operate facilities across state lines. Moore (1996) refers to this as "seamless supervision"—an attempt to reduce confusion when several different regulatory agencies have overlapping jurisdictions.

One example of what these protocols may contain was provided in a May 22, 1996 Federal Reserve Press Release which contained a State/Federal Supervisory Protocol for coordinated supervision of state-chartered interstate banking organizations and a Model Agreement to guide state and federal negotiators attempting to hammer out joint supervisory and examination programs, including the sharing of information useful to all agencies. Each protocol agreement negotiated among regulators in a particular region of the nation would be signed by the regional Federal Reserve Bank or Banks involved, by bank supervisors in the states covered, and possibly the heads of other regulatory agencies also having jurisdiction.

The State-Federal Supervisory Protocol announced in May of 1996 declares that when a state-chartered bank is represented in more than one state, the supervisory agency in the *home state* of that bank will be designated the primary regulator, providing the management and ownership of that bank a single point of contact to get their questions answered. The home state must be responsible for any bank examinations involving its own chartered banks plus taking responsibility to coordinate examinations for its banks with other (host) states where the home state's banks operate facilities and the principal federal supervisor involved. Also, the laws concerning a state-chartered bank's corporate structure and procedures, its charter and bylaws, the rules to be adhered to by its directors and officers, its capitalization and stockholder dividend policies, and the quality of its loans and investments must be set by its home state. However, any other (host) states entered by an out-of-state bank are also expected to play an important role in the areas of antitrust law, deposit concentration limits, regulating branching activity within the host state, insuring protection for consumers of banking services, promoting fair (nondiscriminatory) lending and community development under the terms of recent state/federal protocol agreements. But, each state has the freedom to reshape the recommended May 1996 state/federal protocol to meet its own special regulatory and banking needs and to deal with any special situations faced by the banks it supervises. For example, a bank with branches or affiliated banks in 10 states will probably need a different cooperative federal/state supervisory agreement than a bank represented in only two states.

Overall, the current State-Federal Protocol is aimed at sharing regulatory responsibility for multi-state banks among state and federal supervisors, enhancing interagency coordination and communication. It is also designed to make sure *at least one supervisory agency* is directly accountable to the public and the banks involved and to reassure depository institutions trying to choose between obtaining a state charter or a federal charter of incorporation that each is still a viable choice. Thus, in theory at least, neither federal nor state regulatory systems haven an over-riding advantage over the other. By May of 1996 eleven states in the Western United States—including Alaska, Arizona, California, Hawaii, Idaho, Montana, Nevada, Oregon, Utah, Washington, and Wyoming—and eight states in the eastern portion of the country—including Alabama, Delaware, Maryland, Mississippi, New Jersey, North Carolina, Pennsylvania, and Virginia—had signed agreements that appeared to be generally consistent with the 1996 State/Federal Supervisory Protocol.

Whether these protocols will accomplish all their lofty goals is problematic. There almost certainly will be some gain in the efficient use of supervisory resources and some gain for the bankers being supervised in reducing the burden of regulation. Unfortunately, not enough time has elapsed to evaluate the *de facto* side of these cooperative protocols—how these formal agreements among regulators will actually work out in practice.

Technological change may also profoundly affect regulation by both state and federal authorities and their relative roles within the banking system. Electronic transfers of financial information, including use of the Internet and the World Wide Web, can easily bridge state and national boundaries, even by the smallest banks. Recently a small bank in Pineville, Kentucky went completely online. The traditional concept of a "local community to be served" no longer has the same meaning for a completely electronic bank. Regulators must develop new standards for examining electronic-oriented banks, for assessing their risk exposure, and for evaluating their public-service contributions. The potential for bridging geographic barriers worldwide through electronic networks, even by the smallest banks, suggests that national governments and cooperative agreements among nations, rather than state and local governments, must come to dominate the future regulatory environment for banking.

THE UNFINISHED AGENDA OF BANKING REFORM

Each year the U.S. Congress and the various state legislatures bring forth new calls for deregulation of the American banking industry. The years following passage of the Riegle-Neal interstate banking bill have been no exception. The House Banking Committee, for example, recently promulgated a new law that would allow banks and insurance companies to acquire each other after March 30, 1997, unless prohibited by the individual states (with seventeen states already posting such laws on their books). This proposed bill, authored by House Banking Committee Chairman James Leach (Republican from Iowa), would repeal the provisions of the Glass-Steagall Act separating banks and securities firms; it would permit commercial banks to operate investment banks and allow banks, insurance companies, and securities firms to merge under a common holding company structure.

Banks seem to possess a number of important marketing advantages once they are permitted to sell all types of life and property-casualty insurance. Their network of branch offices gives them a presence in hundreds of local markets. Most banks are already equipped to process payments associated with the collection of insurance premiums and the disbursal of insurance claims. Actually, in the years prior to passage of the Glass-Steagall (National Banking) Act of 1933, many U.S. banks sold insurance, particularly in smaller cities and rural areas. Moreover, leading U.S. banks (including J. P. Morgan & Co., Bankers Trust New York Corp., NationsBank Corp., and thirty-five other U.S. bank holding companies) have already been granted corporate security underwriting powers by the Federal Reserve Board, provided their investment banking services are marketed through a so-called Section 20 subsidiary company.[1] The U.S. banking industry currently is divided on whether or not it wants the Congress to repeal the Glass-Steagall Act out of fear that Congress will do what it did during the 1930s—take away some other valued service power (such as selling and underwriting life and property insurance) in return for granting the industry broader investment banking powers.

If all of these current new-service proposals were ultimately enacted into law, it would fundamentally restructure the whole American financial-services industry, producing even more extensive changes than will follow from the 1994 interstate banking law. Moreover, there have been a wealth of proposed changes in *consumer protection laws* included in recent bills aimed at restructuring the U.S. banking industry. Among the most significant of these heavily promoted changes are:

1. proposed elimination of several of the disclosure rules specified in the Truth in Savings Act of 1991, telling customers *less* about the terms of their deposit relationship with a bank;

2. proposed easing of bank disclosure requirements under Truth in Lending and the Real Estate Settlement Procedures Act for home mortgages and removing or limiting the right of loan recission—that is, the customer's right to back out of a loan agreement within three days of signing it—granted to consumers who have placed their home at risk under the terms of a loan;

3. Proposed elimination of lender liability for pollution or damage of the environment found on foreclosed properties provided the lender is not the direct cause of the pollution, thus allegedly freeing up more bank credit for such businesses as print shops, dry cleaners, automobile repair shops, and other businesses who, potentially at least, could have an adverse impact on the environment; and

4. proposed relaxation of certain rules under the Fair Credit Reporting Act that would allow bank holding companies to share information between their subsidiary firms concerning their customers' personal financial data in order to aid in making better-informed credit and marketing decisions.

Whatever their individual merits, these proposed changes in current U.S. banking law and regulation suggest that Americans are caught up in a period of transition and turmoil in the structure and focus of the banking industry. American banking, more than at any other time in its history, is *not* an established institution; rather it is rapidly becoming something else—something not yet entirely clear to even its keenest observers. Technology is shaking the industry at its roots, reminding bankers daily that their most important service offerings are not simply deposits and loans but intangible service qualities that customers still seem to value highly—trust, safety and security, accurate record keeping, speed of execution, reliability, and transactional convenience. These traditional service qualities are now being packaged and delivered in new forms and through new channels. The challenge American banks have today is to preserve those service qualities customers still value and are willing to pay for, while providing essential services at a cost that remains competitive with the service offerings of a growing list of domestic and foreign competitors.

In short, interstate banking is only *one* manifestation of a structural upheaval that is reshaping American banking from its foundations, albeit it remains an important one. Certainly the time has come for interstate full-service banking to become a reality. However, bankers who are alert, who care, and who wish to compete probably can survive even as small, primarily locally oriented firms operating in the shadow of the industry's interstate giants. Still, all banks of the future—the big and the small—must come to terms with a new order of things, including new organizational forms and new delivery methods. Above all, the survivors in this race for consolidation and change in American banking must be willing to make an unswerving commitment to service quality and service reliability and must develop an alert sensitivity to the ever changing service needs of their customers. It is a challenge truly worthy of the best talent and resources that American banks can attract and hold.

NOTE

1. U.S. bankers seem to be sharply divided over the relative merits of current proposals to repeal the investment banking restrictions in the Glass-Steagall Act, especially if repeal would bring along with it loss of other services the industry would really like to add to its service menu (such as underwriting insurance policies and selling a broader range of insurance coverages). Currently the Federal Reserve Board allows underwriting of so-called ineligible securities (which include most corporate stocks and bonds) so long as this activity is carried out through a separate subsidiary (Section 20 firm) and any revenues from underwriting "ineligible" securities amount to no more than 10 percent of the underwriting subsidiary's total revenues. Many U.S. bankers would probably be happy if the Federal Reserve Board simply raises the 10 percent underwriting revenue cap, perhaps to 15 or 20 percent, without repealing the Glass-Steagall Act and thereby posing a threat to the industry's other service options.

Bibliography

Abrams, Burton A., and Russell F. Settle. "Pressure-Group Influence and Institutional Change: Branch-Banking Legislation During the Great Depression." *Public Choice*, 77 (1993), pp. 687–705.

Akhavein, J. D., A. N. Berger, and D. B. Humphrey. "The Effects of Bank Megamergers on Efficiency and Prices: Evidence from the Profit Function." *Review of Industrial Organization*, 11 (1996).

Alhadeff, David A. *Monopoly and Competition in Banking.* Berkeley: University of California Press, 1954.

Amel, Dean F. "State Laws Affecting the Geographic Expansion of Commercial Banks," *Working Paper.* Board of Governors of the Federal Reserve System, August 1993, pp. 1–42.

Amel, Dean F., and J. Nellie Liang. "The Relationship Between Entry into Banking Markets and Changes in Legal Restrictions on Entry." *Antitrust Bulletin*, XXXVII (Fall 1992), pp. 631–49.

American Bankers' Association. "Interstate Branching: Who's Opting In, Who's Opting Out, Who's Looking at the Options." *ABA Banking Journal*, October 1995, p. 12.

American Bankers' Association. "Call Reports Study by ABA." *American Banker*, April 11, 1996, p. 3.

Anderson, Paul S. "What Price Branching?" *New England Review*, Federal Reserve Bank of Boston, August 1964, pp. 2–9.

Anderson Consulting. *Vision 2000: The Transformation of Banking.* Chicago: Bank Administration Institute, 1994.

Ballen, Robert G., and Joseph P. Savage, "Interstate Branching: Are the Walls Starting to Crumble?" *Banking Law Journal*, III, No. 2 (March/April 1994), pp. 149–72

Bauer, Paul W., and Brian A. Cromwell, "The Effect of Bank Structure and Profitability on Firm Openings," *Economic Review*, Federal Reserve Bank of Cleveland, 4th quarter 1989, pp. 29–37.

Benston, George J. "Branch Banking and Economies of Scale." *Journal of Finance*, XX (May 1965), pp. 312–31.

Berger, A. N., and D. B. Humphrey. "The Dominance of Inefficiencies over Scale and Product Mix Economies in Banking." *Journal of Monetary Economics*, 28 (1991), pp. 117–148.

Berger, Allen N., John H. Leusner, and John J. Mingo, "The Efficiency of Bank Branches and Implications for Mergers and Interstate Branching." In *Proceedings of the Conference on Bank Structure and Competition*. Federal Reserve Bank of Chicago, 1995, pp. 332–347.

Berger, Allen N., and Gregory F. Udell. "Universal Banking and the Future of Small Business Lending," *Working Paper No. 95–17*. The Wharton Financial Institutions Center, University of Pennsylvania, 1995.

Berger, Allen, and Gregory Udell. "Universal Banking and the Future of Small Business Lending." In A. Sanders and I. Walter, editors, *Financial System Design: The Case for Universal Banking*. Burr Ridge, Illinois: Irwin, forthcoming.

Berger, Allen N., Anil K. Rashyap, and Joseph M. Scalise. "The Transformation of the U.S. Banking Industry: What a Long Strange Trip It's Been." *Brookings Papers on Economic Acitivity*, 2 (1995).

Berlin, Mitchell, and Loretta J. Mester. "Financial Intermediation As Vertical Integration," *Working Paper No. 93–3*. Economic Research Division, Federal Reserve Bank of Philadelphia, 1993.

Bernstein, David. "Asset Quality and Scale Economies in Banking." *Journal of Economics and Business*, XLVIII (1996), pp. 157–66.

Black, Harold A., M. Andrew Fields, and Robert L. Schweitzer. "Changes in Interstate Banking Laws: The Impact of Shareholder Wealth." *Journal of Finance*, XLV (1990), pp. 1663–71.

Board of Governors of the Federal Reserve System, State/Federal Supervisory Protocol and Model Agreement, Press Release, May 22, 1996.

Born, Jeffrey A., Robert A. Eisenbeis, and Robert S. Harris. "The Benefits of Geographical and Product Expansion in the Financial Services Industry." *Journal of Financial Services Research*, I (1988), pp. 161–82.

Calem, Paul S. "The Impact of Geographic Deregulation on Small Banks." *Business Review*, Federal Reserve Bank of Philadelphia, November/December 1994, pp. 17–31.

Calem, Paul S., and Leonard I. Nakamura. "Branch Banking and the Geographic Effects on Bank Pricing." *Finance and Economic Discussion Series No. 95–25*. Board of Governors of the Federal Reserve System, May 1995.

Campbell, Carl M., III. "The Effects of State and Industry Economic Conditions on New Firm Entry." *Journal of Economics and Business*, XLVIII (1996), pp. 167–183.

Chapman, John M., and Ray B. Westerfield. *Branch Banking: Its Historical and Theoretical Position in America and Abroad*. New York: Harper and Rowe, 1942.

Clark, Jeffrey. "Economies of Scale and Scope at Depository Financial Institutions: A Review of the Literature." *Economic Review*, Federal Reserve Bank of Kansas City, September/October 1988, pp. 16–33.

Cole, Rebel, and John D. Wolken. "Financial Services Used by Small Businesses: Evidence from the 1993 National Survey of Small Business." *Federal Reserve Bulletin*, 81 (1995), pp. 629–67.

Cyrnak, Anthony W., and Stephen A. Rhoades. "Small Markets: A Potentially Profitable Approach to Geographic Expansion." *Issues in Bank Regulation*, Spring 1989, pp. 21–26.

Darnell, Jerome C. "Banking Structure and Economic Growth." In *Changing Pennsylvania's Branching Laws: An Economic Analysis*. Federal Reserve Bank of Philadelphia, 1973.

De, S., and D. Duplichan. "Effects of Interstate Bank Mergers on Shareholder Wealth: Theory and Evidence." In *Proceedings of the Fourth International Symposium on Money, Banking, and Insurance*. Karlsruhe, Germany, 1987.

De Cossio, F., J. W. Trifts, and K. Scanlon. "Bank Equity Returns: The Difference Between Intrastate and Interstate Bank Mergers." In *Proceedings from a Conference on Bank Structure and Competition*. Federal Reserve Bank of Chicago, 1988.

Dickens, R. N., and J. W. Wansley. "The Impact of Bank Acquisitions: A Comparison of Interstate and Intrastate Mergers," *Working Paper*. Federal Reserve Bank of Philadelphia, 1989.

Dreher, Darrel L., Hugh M. Hayden, and Michael C. Tomkies. "Developments in the Interstate Delivery of Consumer Financial Services." *The Business Lawyer*, May 1995, pp. 1093–108.

Eager, Robert C. "The New Federal Interstate Banking and Branching Legislation." *The Bankers Magazine*, November/December 1995, pp. 23–28.

Economides, Nicholas, R. Glenn Hubbard, and Darius Palia. "The Political Economy of Branching Restrictions and Deposit Insurance," *Working Paper*. New York University, 1993.

Eisenbeis, Robert A. "Economic and Policy Issues Surrounding Regional and National Approaches to Interstate Banking." In *Dynamics of Banking*. Arlington Heights, Illinois: Davidson, Inc., 1985.

Eisenbeis, R. A., R. S. Harris, and J. Lakonishok. "Benefits of Bank Diversification: The Evidence from Shareholder Returns." *Journal of Finance*, XXXIX (1987), pp. 881–92.

Ellishausen, G. E., and J. D. Wolken. "Banking Markets and the Use of Financial Services by Small and Medium-Sized Businesses." *Federal Reserve Bulletin*, October 1990, pp. 801–17.

Engel, James. "Federal Institutions Enter the Brave New World of State and Local Taxation." *The Bankers Magazine*, November/December 1995, pp. 36–41.

Fant, Julian E. "Small Banks' Strengths and Weaknesses." In *Interstate Banking Strategies for a New Era*. Westport, Connecticut: Quorum Books and Greenwood Press, 1985.

Faulhaber, Gerald R. "Banking Markets: Productivity, Risk, and Customer Satisfaction," *Working Paper No. 95–15*. The Wharton Financial Institutions Center, The University of Pennsylvania, 1995.

Federal Deposit Insurance Corporation. *Statistics on Banking*. Washington, D.C., 1994.

Federal Deposit Insurance Corporation. *The FDIC Quarterly Banking Profile.* Washington, D.C., 1st quarter 1996.

Federal Reserve Bank of Minneapolis. *Fedgazette,* VI, No. 3 (July 1994).

Federal Reserve Board. *Annual Report, 1995.*

Frieder, Larry, Vincent Apilado, George Benston, Jeffrey Davis, Robert Eisenbeis, Thomas Gies, Paul Horvitz, Harvey Rosenblum, and David Whitehead, III. *Commercial Banking and Interstate Expansion: Issues, Prospects, and Strategies.* Ann Arbor, Michigan: UMI Research Press, 1985.

Furlong, Fred, and Gary C. Zimmerman. "Consolidation California Style." *FRBSF Weekly Letter,* Federal Reserve Bank of San Francisco, 95–36 (October 27, 1995), pp. 1–2.

Goldberg, Lawrence G., and Gerald A. Hanweck. "What Can We Expect from Interstate Banking?" *Journal of Banking and Finance,* XII (1988), pp. 51–67.

Goldberg, Lawrence G., Gerald A. Hanweck, and Timothy F. Sugure. "Differential Impact on Bank Valuation of Interstate Banking Law Changes." *Journal of Banking and Finance,* 1992, pp. 1143–58.

Greenspan, Alan. "Remarks at Dedication Ceremonies for a Chair in Banking and Monetary Economics, Wartburg College, Waverly, Iowa." Board of Governors of the Federal Reserve System, May 6, 1994.

Hannan, Timothy H., and Stephen A. Rhoades. "Future U.S. Banking Structure: 1990 to 2010." *The Antitrust Bulletin,* Fall 1992, pp. 737–98.

Hunter, W. C., and S. G. Timme. "Technological Change in Large U.S. Commercial Banks," *Journal of Business,* LXIV (1991), pp. 339–62.

Hunter, W. C., S. G. Timme, and Won Keun Yang. "An Examination of Cost Subadditivity and Multi-product Production in Large U.S. Banks." *Journal of Money, Credit, and Banking,* 1990, pp. 504–25.

Indick, Murray A. "Considerations for Interstate Banking Transactions." *The Bankers Magazine,* November/December 1995, pp. 3–5.

Indick, Murray A., and Satish M. Kini, "The Interstate Banking and Branching Efficiency Act: New Options, New Problems," *Banking Law Journal,* 112, No. 2 (February 1995), pp. 100–23.

Jackson, William E. "Is the Market Well Defined in Bank Merger and Acquistion Analysis?" *Review of Economics and Statistics,* LXXIV (November 1992), pp. 655–61.

Jayarantne, Jith, and Philip E. Strahn. "The Finance-Growth Nexus: Evidence from Bank Branch Deregulation," *Research Paper 95–13.* Federal Reserve Bank of New York, June 1995.

Kane, Edward J. "De Jure Interstate Banking: Why Only Now?" *Working Paper No. 95–40.* Wallace E. Carroll School of Management, Boston College, April 1995.

Keeton, William R. "Multi-Office Bank Lending to Small Businesses: Some New Evidence." *Economic Review,* Federal Reserve Bank of Kansas City, 2nd quarter 1995, pp. 45–57.

Keeton, William R. "Do Bank Mergers Reduce Lending to Businesses and Farmers? New Evidence from the Tenth District States," *Economic Review,* Federal Reserve Bank of Kansas City, Third Quarter 1996, pp. 63–75.

Kelley, Edward W., Jr. Speech to the 20th National Conference on Banking, American Institute of Certified Public Accountants. Washington, D.C., November 16, 1995.

Laderman, Elizabeth. "The Rhyme and Reason of Bank Mergers." *FRBSF Weekly Letter*, Federal Reserve Bank of San Francisco, 95–39 (November 17, 1995).

Laderman, Elizabeth S., and Randall S. Pozdena. "Interstate Banking and Competition: Evidence from the Behavior of Stock Returns." *Economic Review*, Federal Reserve Bank of San Francisco, Spring 1991, pp. 32–47.

LaWare, John P. Testimony before the Subcommittee on Financial Institutions Supervision, Regulation, and Deposit Insurance of the Committee on Banking, Finance, and Urban Affairs, U.S. House of Representatives, June 22, 1993.

Lee, William. "Bank Diversification: The Value of Risk Reduction to Investors and the Potential for Reducing Required Capital." *Excess Capacity in the Financial Sector*, Federal Reserve Bank of New York, June 1993, pp. 59–89.

Levonian, Mark E. "Interstate Banking and Risk." *Weekly Letter*, Federal Reserve Bank of San Francisco, 94–26 (July 22, 1994), pp. 1–2.

Levonian, Mark E., and Jennifer Solder. "Small Banks, Small Loans, Small Business." *FRBSF Weekly Letter*, Federal Reserve Bank of San Francisco, 96–02 (January 12, 1996), pp. 1–3.

Liang, Nellie, and Stephen A. Rhoades. "Geographic Diversification and Risk in Banking." *Journal of Economics and Business*, XLV (1988), pp. 271–84.

McAllister, Patrick H., and Douglas A. McManus. *Diversification and Risk in Banking: Evidence from ExPost Returns*. Finance and Economics Discussion Series No. 201. Washington, D.C.; Board of Governors of the Federal Reserve System, June 1992.

McAllister, P. H., and D. McManus. "Resolving the Scale Efficiency Puzzle in Banking." *Journal of Banking and Finance*, XVII (1993), pp. 389–406.

McLaughlin, Susan. "The Impact of Interstate Banking and Branching Reform from the States." *Current Issues in Economics and Finance*, Federal Reserve Bank of New York, I (May 1995).

Marcus, Alan. "Deregulation and Bank Financial Policy." *Journal of Banking and Finance*, 1984, pp. 557–65.

Merrick, William, "Interstate Banking May Increase Competition." *Credit Union Magazine*, LXI, No. 6 (June 1995), p. 14.

Millon-Cornett, M., and S. De. "Common Stock Returns in Corporate Takeover Bids: Evidence of Interstate Bank Mergers." *Journal of Banking and Finance*. XV (1991), pp. 23–29.

Millon-Cornett, M. and H. Tehranian, "Changes in Corporate Performance Associated with Bank Acquisitions," *Journal of Financial Economics*, XXXI (1992), pp. 211–234.

Moore, R. Chris. "Interstate Banking Will Bring Changes in Fed Regulatory Practices," *Focus*, Federal Reserve Bank of Cleveland, Second Quarter 1996, pp. 1–2.

Moore, Robert R. "Does Geographic Liberalization Really Hurt Small Banks?" *Financial Industry Studies*, Federal Reserve Bank of Dallas, December 1995, pp. 1–12.

Moore, Robert R., and Karen Couch. "Have Small Banks Been Caught Off-Balance?" *Financial Industry Studies*, Federal Reserve Bank of Dallas, December 1994, pp. 13–23.

Mote, Larry R. "The Perennial Issue: Branch Banking." *Business Conditions,* Federal Reserve Bank of Chicago, February 1974, pp. 3–23.

Nadler, Paul S. "Why the Present Surge in the Bankers' Urge to Merge?" *The Secured Lender,* LI, No. 5 (September/October 1995), pp. 24–28.

Nakamura, Leonard I. "Commercial Bank Information: Implications for the Structure of Banking." In Michael Klausner and Lawrence J. White, editors, *Structural Change in Banking.* Homewood, Illinois: Business One/Irwin, 1993.

Noulas, Athanasios, Subhash Ray, and Stephen Miller. "Returns to Scale and Input Substitution for Large U.S. Banks." *Journal of Money, Credit, and Banking,* 1990, pp. 94–108.

Peek, Joe, and Eric Rosengren. "The Effects of Interstate Branching on Small Business Lending." In *Proceedings of the Conference on Bank Structure and Competition,* Federal Reserve Bank of Chicago, 1995, pp. 314–324.

Peek, Joe, and Eric Rosengren. "Small Business Credit Availability: How Important Is the Size of the Lender?" In A. Saunders and Ingo Walter, editors, *Universal Banking: Financial System Designs Reconsidered.* Burr Ridge, Illinois: Irwin, 1996.

Petersen, Mitchell A., and Raghunam G. Rajan. "The Benefits of Lending Relationships: Evidence from the Small Business Data," *Journal of Finance,* 49 (1994), pp. 3–37.

Rhoades, Stephen A. "A Note on the Resource-Allocation Efficiency of MBHCs Versus Independent Banks." *Quarterly Review of Economics and Business,* Summer 1983.

Rhoades, Stephen A. "Consolidation of the Banking Industry and the Merger Guidelines." *Antitrust Bulletin,* Fall 1992, pp. 689–705.

Rhoades, Stephen A. "Interstate Banking and Product-Line Expansion: Implications from Available Evidence." *Loyola of Los Angeles Law Review,* XVIII, No. 4 (1985).

Rhoades, Stephen A. "Mergers and Acquisitions by Commercial Banks, 1980–1994," *Staff Study.* Federal Reserve Board, 4th quarter 1995.

Rose, John T. "Interstate Banking and Small Business Finance: Implications from Available Evidence." *American Journal of Small Business,* Fall 1986, pp. 23–39.

Rose, John T., and Donald T. Savage. "Interstate Banking and the Viability of Small, Independent Banks: Further Evidence on Market Share Accumulation by New Banks." *The Antitrust Bulletin,* Winter 1987, pp. 1001–18.

Rose, John T., and John D. Wolken. "Geographic Diversification in Banking, Market Share Changes and the Viability of Small Independent Banks." *Journal of Financial Services Research,* IV (March 1990), pp. 5–20.

Rose, Peter S. *The Changing Structure of American Banking.* New York: Columbia University Press, 1987.

Rose, Peter S. *The Interstate Banking Revolution: Benefits, Risks, and Tradeoffs for Bankers and Consumers.* Westport, Connecticut: Quorum Books, 1989.

Rose, Peter S. "The Banking Firms Making Interstate Acquisitions: Theory and Observable Motives." *Review of Business and Economic Research,* XXV, No. 1 (Fall 1989a), pp. 1–18.

Rose, Peter S. "The Firms Acquired by Interstate Banks: Testable Hypotheses and

Consistent Evidence." *Journal of Business and Economic Perspectives*, XV, No. 1 (Fall 1989b), pp. 127–136.

Rose, Peter S. "Interstate Banking: Performance, Market Share, and Market Concentration Issues." *The Antitrust Bulletin*, XXXVII, No. 3 (Fall 1992), pp. 601–30.

Rose, Peter S. "Diversification and Interstate Banking." *The New Tool Set: Assessing Innovations in Banking*, 31st Annual Conference on Bank Structure and Competition, May 1995, pp. 296–313.

Rose, Peter S. *Commercial Bank Management*. 3rd ed. Chicago: Richard D. Irwin, Inc., 1996a.

Rose, Peter S. "Diversification and Cost Effects of Interstate Banking." *The Financial Review*. XXXIII, No. 2 (May 1996b).

Savage, Donald T. "Interstate Banking: A Status Report." *Federal Reserve Bulletin*, December 1993, pp. 1075–89.

Schilling, Tim. "The (Inter) State of Banking." *On Reserve*, Federal Reserve Bank of Chicago, 31 (April 1995), pp. 1–3.

Siems, Thomas F. "Bank Mergers and Shareholder Wealth: Evidence from 1995's Megamerger Deals." *Financial Industry Studies*, Federal Reserve Bank of Dallas, August 1996, pp. 1–12.

Smith, Brian W., and Timothy E. Keehen, "Hostile Bids and Interstate Banking: Is Your Bank Ready?" *The Bankers Magazine*, November/December 1995, pp. 29–35.

Sommer, Joseph H. "The American Origin of the Separation of Banking and Commerce," *Research Paper No. 9309*. Federal Reserve Bank of New York, July 1993.

Spiegel, John W., and Alan Gart, "What Lies Behind the Bank Merger and Acquisition Frenzy." *Business Economics*, April 1996, pp. 47–52.

Spong, Kenneth. *Banking Regulation: Its Purposes, Implementation and Effects*. Federal Reserve Bank of Kansas City, 1994.

Spong, Kenneth, and J. D. Shoenhair. "Performance of Banks Acquired on an Interstate Basis." *Financial Industry Perspectives*, Federal Reserve Bank of Kansas City, December 1992, pp. 15–23.

Spong, Kenneth, Richard J. Sullivan, and Robert DeYoung. "What Makes a Bank Efficient? A Look at Financial Characteristics and Management and Ownership Structure." *Financial Industry Perspectives*, Federal Reserve Bank of Kansas City, December 1995, pp. 1–20.

Sprague, O. M. W. "Branch Banking in the United States." *Quarterly Journal of Economics*, XVII (February 1993), pp. 242–60.

Stigler, George J. "The Theory of Economic Regulation." *Bell Journal of Economics and Management Science*, II (Spring 1971), pp. 3–21.

Stock, Stuart C., and Mark E. Plotkin. "A Summary of the New Interstate Banking Act." *Review of Banking and Financial Services*, XI (January 1995), pp. 11–18.

Strahan, Philip E., and James Weston, "Small Business Lending and Bank Consolidation: Is There Cause for Concern?" *Current Issues in Economics and Finance*, Federal Reserve Bank of New York, II, No. 3 (March 1996), pp. 1–6.

Sullivan, Richard J., and Kenneth Spong. "Successful Strategies in Interstate Bank

Acquisitions." *Financial Industry Perspectives*, Federal Reserve Bank of Kansas City, December 1995, pp. 21–37.

Tart, Charlotte L. "Expansion of the Banking Industry Under the Riegle-Neal Interstate Banking Efficiency Act of 1994: Is the Banking Industry Headed in the Right Direction?" *Wake Forest Law Review*, XXX, No. 4 (Winter 1995), pp. 915–49.

Taylor, Bruce W. "Industry Consolidation and the Endurance of Community Banking." *The Bankers Magazine*, November/December 1995, pp. 42–44.

Taylor, Jeremy F. "Forward Valuation in Banking." *The Bankers Magazine*, November/December 1995, pp. 45–49.

Tirabassi, Salvatore. "Riegle-Neal, Glass-Steagall, and Consolidation." *The Bankers Magazine*, November/December 1995, pp. 50–53.

Trifts, Jack W., and Kevin P. Scanlon. "Interstate Bank Mergers: The Early Evidence." *The Journal of Financial Research*, X, No. 4 (Winter 1987), pp. 305–311.

U.S. General Accounting Office. "Interstate Banking Benefits and Risks of Removing Regulatory Restrictions." Washington, D.C., November 1993.

U.S. Treasury Department. *Modernizing the Financial System: Recommendations for Safer, More Competitive Banks*. Washington, D.C., 1991.

Whalen, Gary. "Out-of-State Holding Company Affiliation and Small Business Lending," *Comptroller of the Currency Economic and Policy Analysis Working Paper No. 95–4.* 1995.

Yellen, Janet L. Testimony before the Subcommittee on Financial Institutions and Consumer Credit. U.S. House of Representatives, October 17, 1995.

Index

About the Author

PETER S. ROSE is Professor of Finance and Jeanne and John R. Blocker Professor of Business Administration at Texas A&M University. After serving as a financial economist with the Federal Reserve System, Dr. Rose turned to teaching more than two decades ago. He is author of nearly 200 articles and numerous scholarly books, textbooks, and other teaching materials, including *Japanese Banking and Investment in the United States* (1991) and *The Interstate Banking Revolution* (1989), both from Quorum.